S0-AIO-988

| | | | |
|---|---|---|---|
| | | | |
| | | | |
| | | | |
| | | | |
| | | | |
| | | | |
| | | | |
| | | | |
| | | | |
| | | | |
| | | | |
| | | | |

THE

# Walter Clinton Jackson Essays

IN THE SOCIAL SCIENCES

# THE
# Walter Clinton Jackson
# Essays
# IN THE SOCIAL SCIENCES

By

MEMBERS OF THE FACULTY
OF THE WOMAN'S COLLEGE OF THE
UNIVERSITY OF NORTH CAROLINA

Edited by

VERA LARGENT

*Essay Index Reprint Series*

BOOKS FOR LIBRARIES PRESS
FREEPORT, NEW YORK

First Published 1942

Reprinted 1972 by arrangement with
The University of North Carolina Press.



Library of Congress Cataloging in Publication Data

North Carolina. University. Woman's College, Greensboro.
The Walter Clinton Jackson essays in the social sciences.

(Essay index reprint series)
"Published upon the occasion of the fiftieth anniversary of the founding of the Woman's College of the University of North Carolina."
Reprint of the 1942 ed.
Includes bibliographical references.
1. Social sciences--Addresses, essays, lectures.
I. Largent, Vera Ione, ed. II. Title.
[H35.N6 1972] 300'.8 79-167431
ISBN 0-8369-2725-7

PRINTED IN THE UNITED STATES OF AMERICA
BY
NEW WORLD BOOK MANUFACTURING CO., INC.
HALLANDALE, FLORIDA 33009

PUBLISHED

UPON THE OCCASION OF

THE FIFTIETH ANNIVERSARY

OF THE FOUNDING OF

THE WOMAN'S COLLEGE OF THE

UNIVERSITY OF NORTH CAROLINA

TO

Dean Walter Clinton Jackson

GREAT TEACHER

HIS FRIENDS AND COLLEAGUES DEDICATE THIS VOLUME IN RECOGNITION OF THE VISION AND ENTHUSIASM WHICH HAVE MADE POSSIBLE THE PLACE NOW HELD BY THE SOCIAL SCIENCES AT THE WOMAN'S COLLEGE OF THE UNIVERSITY OR NORTH CAROLINA

# Editorial Acknowledgments

TOO MANY of my colleagues to mention by name have made possible the completion of this work by their criticisms, their suggestions, and their encouragement. Their help I deeply appreciate. I wish especially to express my sincere gratitude to Dr. Benjamin Burks Kendrick, whose valuable critical assistance and steady interest in the project have been invaluable; to Dr. Elizabeth Cometti, who has given unselfishly of her time and generously of her skill; to Dr. Winfield Rogers, who gave me the benefit of his literary judgment; and to Miss Jane Summerell, Faculty Chairman of the Fiftieth Anniversary Committee, and Miss Rachel Clifford, its Executive Secretary. I also wish to thank Miss Magnhilde Gullander, Miss Bernice Draper, and Mr. C. D. Johns, who shared with me the dull task of reading proof.

VERA LARGENT

# Editorial Acknowledgments

Many of my colleagues too numerous to mention by name have made possible the completion of this work by their criticisms [illegible] judgment. [illegible] I wish especially to express my sincere gratitude [illegible] [illegible] [illegible] [illegible] [illegible] [illegible] [illegible] [illegible]

# Contents

# Introduction

*VERA LARGENT*
*Associate Professor of History*

*These are the times that try men's Souls. . . . Tyranny, like hell, is not easily conquered; yet we have this consolation with us, that the harder the conflict the more glorious the triumph. What we obtain too cheap, we esteem too lightly; 'tis dearness that gives everything its value.*—Thomas Paine, *The Crisis.* December, 1776.

THE AUTHORS of these studies, members of the faculty of The Woman's College of the University of North Carolina, have differing points of view as to the relative importance of the various social sciences, indeed as to how wide is the range of subject matter which can properly be included under the social sciences. But they have two things in common: a concern with democracy as a way of life and with its successes or failures in the region, the nation, and the world; and a conviction that at The Woman's College the democratic ideal has been wisely fostered by the faculty of the social sciences and has been stimulated in the students sent out to practice it as individuals in the strife of modern life. Moreover, they are never forgetful of the fact that the rôle of the social sciences on this campus has taken form largely under the vigorous and truly democratic leadership of Dr. Walter Clinton Jackson—from 1909 to 1932, as Head of the Department of History, Head of the Department of History and Economics, and Chairman of the Faculty of Social Science; and since 1934, as Dean of Administration. In these later years his interest in the social sciences has continued as he has guided the task of broadening and enriching the curriculum of the college. It is fitting, therefore, that on the fiftieth anniversary of the founding of The Woman's College such a volume as this should appear.

It is proper in a democracy that in times like these, times

which "try men's souls," a group of individuals bound together by work and exchange of ideas should consider problems of common interest, each approaching his problem from his own particular point of view and in terms of his own particular discipline. Thus we pass, in turn, from the past to the present, from the subjective to the objective, from the philosophical to the concrete, from the region to the world, in our search for those truths which we as individuals may hold in the United States. This privilege we do not "esteem too lightly" for we have not obtained it "too cheap." And those who write are united in the hope that their work may be of some value in stimulating other free minds to build that defense of opinion, well considered and firmly believed, which will become the best offense against tyranny.

From the Era of Napoleon and the War of 1812 until the last decades of the nineteenth century the watchword of European and American liberals was freedom—freedom of speech, of press, of religion, of person, freedom to control one's own business with a minimum of state interference. The Jeffersonian ideal of "the less government the better" might have been productive of a Utopia had all citizens been paragons of civic virtue, had they, like Rousseau's ideal citizens, always been willing to subordinate personal welfare to the general will and conscientiously to work for the general welfare. But in nineteenth-century Europe and America, "freedom" became too often freedom from control in the interests of the general welfare if that control conflicted with individual gain, even freedom to exploit others without interference from the agency of the people, the government. This was not democracy in any true sense of the word. Nor was it freedom of the sort that could, under modern capitalism, accomplish the aim of the early liberals, "the greatest happiness of the greatest number."

As the century passed into its later decades, democracy replaced freedom as the slogan and as the Utopia of the progressives. And in democracy the emphasis was upon equality—equality of opportunity for the poor with the rich, for women with men, for Negroes with whites—and upon security, both social-economic and political. Not that freedom was scorned. Instead, the idea was extended to include a belief that, since individuals have misused freedom, the truest freedom is to be found in a state in which the government, chosen by a majority of the free citizens, is an active agent for the protection of the basic freedoms and of that equality of opportunity and equality under the law which is necessary to human happiness. Napoleon once said, "Freedom is the need of a class that is not very numerous and is privileged by circumstances; equality, on the other hand, is what pleases the crowd."[1] But that was the word of a cynical dictator, of one who had no respect for the people or their rule. The idea of the modern democrat was rather that of Katharine Lee Bates, author of *America the Beautiful*, who wrote, "Confirm thy soul in self-control, thy liberty in law"; or of Rousseau, who pointed out that the sovereign people who delegate certain powers to their government and submit to certain controls by it are not giving up their individual liberties in so doing, since the government is created by them and will, if they are responsible citizens, act only in accord with the general will. To surrender rights, liberties, to the government is to give them up to themselves, the sovereigns.[2] And today, when Mr. Roosevelt speaks of the "four freedoms," he is speaking of that freedom which is based upon equality and which can be guaranteed only by strong governments directed by citizens who are ever aware of their responsibilities.

The authors of the essays in this volume agree that the greatest weakness of democracy has been the concern of citizens with their rights—with freedom in the early, limited selfish sense—to the exclusion of their responsibilities, and that its greatest strength lies in its resiliency and in the self-confidence and the coöperation of which disciplined, aware citizens are capable. As Tapiola says in his soliloquy at the end of the war which he and his "brave regiment" have waged,

For if freedom is a thistle full of pains, it is never-the-less a lovely flower, and the fields would be bare and dismal without it.... We must fight for the thistle, but we must not cry out when it stings us.[3]

At The Woman's College of the University of North Carolina the basic academic freedoms—of speech, of writing, of teaching—have always been respected and protected. Faculty members have been respected as individuals and their right, indeed their duty, to teach the truth, as they know it, has been jealously guarded. Students also have had, for many years, the right of self-government with its training for responsible citizenship. They have always had the right of petition and, as years have passed, have assumed more and more the responsibilities of community citizenship, until today there is no problem involving student life, academic or social, which students may not help solve. That "Responsible Freedom" is the motto of student government is not lacking in significance. Here students learn to make decisions independently and to bear the stings of failure, which can be turned into success if courage and persistence are great enough. Here they learn the fundamentals of a living democracy: that they must as citizens be willing to forego some personal, individual gains, that they must think in terms of the general welfare while jealously guarding their individualism. If "freedom is a thistle," students who have passed through The Woman's College of the University of North Carolina and who have studied the social sciences should also realize its loveliness and the possibility of its acquisition.

# A Rich Cargo

*HARRIET ELLIOTT*
*Dean of Women and Professor of Political Science*

"BRETHREN, ye have been called unto liberty, therefore hold your hold, brethren—pull up well upon the oars, you have a rich cargo, and I hope we shall escape shipwreck—daylight and good piloting will secure all." So spoke the Reverend John Wise in the year 1710. And those were crisis days, too, in theocratic New England, where the seeds of a new nation dedicated to the equality of men were struggling to grow out of the night and the ideals of Europe's unwanted.

We pray for daylight and good piloting in the twentieth century. The forms of darkness and the confusions of purpose threatening us today are not those that tried the strength and purpose of those first children of enlightenment who forged the concepts of the freedoms. But the Nazi challenge is not the first that democracy has faced. The living concept of man's freedom and his worth has always battled its way to growth.

For three hundred years America has been fashioning a way of life that stands for something unique in the history of the world; this way is rooted in a belief in man and in his inherent right to "light" and opportunity. To the countless disinherited of Europe, the thought of America brought full-bodied hopes, which no amount of hardship could dispel. In America, the saga ran, was a world which was, and could be, more surely fashioned after the heart's desire. There one might be free. There opportunity was limited only by the cunning of the hand and the ingenuity of the brain. There one might read, and learn, and think. There one could live, not solely on the shadowy anticipations of another world, but could share in the substance of material things in the midst of this fruitful earth.

Not that this way of life would hold for all, nor would the hope be completely realized. On the contrary, for many, in the early days, America was no more than a dismal and impenetrable wilderness wherein exhausting toil was daily companion to the specter of famine and the hovering fear of Indian wars. Romantic as much of it doubtless was, in many respects life on the American frontier was sordid, lonely, and miserable almost beyond the capacity of modern readers to understand. But frontiersmen knew.

They knew that the life was hard for all, and that it bore especially hard on the women. The reality that surrounded their lives on the frontiers was less one of heroism—and there was plenty of that—than of untold and unsung sorrow, bitterness, despair, and perhaps untimely death. The working day led far into the night. Children came with the regularity of the years, and death for both children and mothers was frequent. With the women, as with the men, the daily grind stretched unbroken to the last horizon. Rolvaag's story of Per Hansa's mad wife lost to her eerie fancies in the darkness of her sod hut, placed so precariously on the surface of the boundless western prairies, is history. It summarizes in a single poignant picture the bleakness and agony of countless lives stretched out on the bitter rack of the frontier.

Not much better is the picture of America for many of those late-comers dumped abruptly into the scrofulous slums of our eastern cities, bled white by the speed-up and long hours in sweatshops or factories, or compelled to wander, like social pariahs, from rubbish heap to rubbish heap in the rich crop areas in the West. Ruskin's devastating portrayal of Turner's *Slave Ship* is matched by Upton Sinclair's *The Jungle;* the disasters of Jamestown, by those of tenement fires, Homestead, and Bisbee.

But despite all this, the record was freighted with high promise. What the present might not offer, the future could be made to provide. Belief remained strong that what was bad could soon be bettered; that what was wrong could, before the end, be righted. However black the disasters, despite all reverses through the years, America remained a land of myth and song, a fabled Atlantis of riches and adventure, promising genuine release from the ancient shackles, the hope of life with a bright unfolding future. America has meant these things to untold thousands. And here, despite all the failures and hardships, was, at length, a solid core of continued achievement, in line with the notions that brought our ancestors over. Here the newcomers found, by and large, more real independence, more certain freedom, more definite rights, and a larger backlog of genuine opportunity, than in the lands whence they came. Here they found a more clearly accepted belief in the dignity of labor, and for the most part no man need step humbly from the path if another more haughty passed by.

Almost from the beginning women have been freer than in the Old World. Children have had a larger chance and a wider range of opportunities ahead of them. For the rank and file, education has been easier to acquire on any given level. The arts and sciences have been more open to all. Here, for most, the doors to a different, a more comfortable, a better life have not been closed, in theory; and, for most, they have been, to some degree or other, open in fact. There has been more opportunity to go up in the social, the economic, the political scale. There have been fewer closed social registers and practically no traditions of exclusive hereditary privileges.

It makes little difference what aspect of living one has in mind, with what European country comparison be made, or whether the contrast relate to the early, the middle, or the later periods of American history. In terms of freedom of movement, freedom of speech and expression, standards of living, wage scales, opportunities to vote and hold office, or almost any other aspect, life in America has offered more for the vast mass of the population than for the corresponding social strata in any European country. And the strength and quality of the democratic tradition in America lies in the fact that the old stubborn dream of freedom still lives. Submerged in places and at times, it appears again with renewed vigor. The democratic outlook is not dead, not even dying. Rather is it still near its youth, with its major battles lying just ahead.

In sharp contradistinction to the outlook of distant European ancestors, Americans believe profoundly that "something can be done about it." It is "in their blood" that events are wrought by man, not by forces beyond the control of man. "Somebody is to blame"; this they take for granted—some person, some association of people, or some set of institutions. Then if what is "wrong" can be ascribed to human contrivances, it is man-made; and, being so fashioned, it can be recut and shaped along new lines and in the service of more directly social ends.

Of all the countries in the civilized world, America has had more "dangerous thoughts"; and not only more "dangerous thoughts," more "idle and fanciful dreams" of the future, more traditions of potential worldly bounty, but also more fulfillment and more proof of the possibilities of fulfillment. Nowhere else in the world, at any time in human history, or on any such scale, has the fact of advancement from the lowest to the highest, of change from the meanest and most poverty-stricken condition to one of relative ease and plenty been so common an experience as in the United States. Dreams which come true, even if but partially, become immensely powerful social stimulants by communion with reality. The force of this tradition in American history, this traditional communion of dream and reality cannot be overestimated.

The threat of the thoughts, hopes, and dreams of Americans is a powerful reality to the reactionary forces of the

Nazi-controlled countries, and has led the totalitarians to crush democratic upsurgings in conquered lands. If they do not rule now, their overripe oligarchies must finally be wiped out. Thus it is no accident that in both Italy and Germany, all effort is concentrated on the *Weltanschauung*. Only the totalitarians have grasped in general the potentialities of undemocratic social contrasts; for Americans, living now, find it difficult to appreciate how low their own origins were. Most history—and that of Europe is no exception—chronicles only the fortunes of the upper classes, and hence does not touch on the lives of the vast majority of our American ancestry. Yet 80 to 90 per cent of the people living on this continent today have nothing behind them but a shadowy past. So far as most historians are concerned, the lives and fortunes of this ancestry moved perpetually in a twilight zone of unimportance.

English, French, German; north European and south European; at the beginning or at the end of the grand cycle, the story was essentially the same. The vast majority of the immigrants fled from poverty-stricken and slatternly countrysides, from wretchedly long hours, starvation wages, and the futureless economic slavery of scabrous factory towns, from a gray expanse of years crowded with an inescapable round of exacting and capriciously imposed duties. Social oppression was the companion piece to their poverty and bound them to class status, occupation, and locale, generation after generation: fixity of status, fixity of occupation, fixity of residence.

These oppressed found that opportunity in the New World was greatly superior to that of the old. But, far more significantly, in the New World they learned to believe in the right of every man to opportunity, and so to believe in, at the same time that they experienced, the power of mankind to cut, shape, hew, and master physical environment. They found, in short, an unoccupied virgin continent at a time when the ideas of the Enlightenment were gaining hold on the mentality and institutions of the Western World, and in the course of three hundred years they developed the continent under the stimulus and with the aid of a protean industrial technique. The combination is unique in history. The results can be shown to be far more revolutionizing than most Americans will readily believe—revolutionizing not only in the past, but destined to be far more so in the future.

In the English and French writers of the Enlightenment, Americans found a philosophy ideally adapted to conditions in the New World. Hence, as philosophical ideas developed, they were taken over by the colonists with the greatest enthusiasm. Locke, Hume, and Adam Smith, Voltaire and Rousseau, Diderot and d'Alembert, Condorcet and Condillac were eagerly read and pondered. "Dare to use your understanding," in the words of Emmanuel Kant, "became the motto of the Enlightenment," and comprehension of the natural world was seen as first step in the mastery of its resources. And it was precisely the will to master seemingly limitless natural resources which dominated American psychology in nearly every walk of life.

The spirit of the Enlightenment did not stop, however, with the natural world. It turned its analytical tools loose on social institutions, and the theory of natural rights became for democratic institutions what the theory of natural law was for science and technology. The antecedents of the Enlightenment, including the stimuli which led to the exploratory efforts of the fourteenth and fifteenth centuries (of which the discovery of this continent was a mere by-product), are the antecedents of America. From Roger Williams and Anne Hutchinson to Benjamin Franklin, Thomas Paine, Thomas Jefferson, and Samuel Adams, the intellectual currents that dissolved the autocratic hierarchies of the Old World were gaining ground on the Atlantic frontier.

These intellectual currents gained ground over here far more rapidly than in the Old World, precisely because they were better fitted to the blend of interests and opportunities which dominated life on this side. The French Revolution gave way to Napoleon and to the great reaction known as the Age of Metternich. But while the American Revolution was also succeeded by reaction, the halting of democratic forces here was short-lived. With the triumph of Jefferson, the course for the future was set. Despite numerous reactions thereafter Jeffersonian social philosophy, in the main, never lost its hold on America.

That is to say, while the ideas of the Enlightenment in Europe ran head-on into powerfully entrenched reactionary forces long before they had had a chance to filter throughout the structure of society, in America the strength of the reaction was watered down and thinned out to the point where it was never able for long to obtain full command of the American system. Throughout American history the ferment of democratic doctrines has led to legislation and organization which have, sometimes slowly and sometimes swiftly but always cumulatively, modified the machinery of society on behalf of the majority.

Nevertheless, the forces of democracy might not have gained such tremendous impetus on this continent had it not been for the presence of seemingly inexhaustible resources—first, of lands and forests and minerals and practically every single raw material necessary for the development of a complicated industrial civilization; and secondly, the resources of science and technology. The rise of America parallels the rise of modern science to its fullest development; the spread of American civilization over the land has been paced by the unfolding of industrial technology. Significantly enough, each new concession on the democratic front has been associated with further steps into the expanding frontier, with discovery of new lands and resources, with new and intellectually revolutionary discoveries in the realm of science, and with new applications of industrial technique to the workaday tasks of the world. Amongst all the great industrial countries, this timing is unique to America. The confluence of these trends is peculiar to the unfolding of national consciousness on this continent. Nowhere else is the blending the same.

This confluence, this timing, lent wings to the spread of democratic ideas. But it also gave them a peculiar cast. On the whole, victory came easily. Gains made by popular forces in pursuit of the manifold of conditions and privileges known as democracy were not had without struggle, but they came with sufficient ease and regularity to seem natural. Change in the conditions of life was a daily experience, and change in the institutions that govern social relationships could be achieved by taking the appropriate action. From the days of the agitation over the Bill of Rights to the present, the people believed they could win at need. By common consent all that was required was that the people organize, mass their strength, vote the right way.

Therefore the mood throughout was essentially optimistic, at times was bombastically so. Victory was taken for granted. The material world had been, was being, and could be made to yield the tangible requirements of the "good life." So could the proud and dictatorial be humbled now, as they had been brought low in the past. Everything was possible to the cunning and the brave. The world was theirs.

The mood was likewise extremely opportunistic. To an increasing extent with the passage of years, democratic ideas became clichés, slogans for the moment. The very swiftness with which the population was spread out over the land favored intellectual decadence. So likewise did the spectacular unfolding of industrial technology, the rapid growth of new industries, new types of organization, and a million other changes in the kaleidoscope of the American scene. In many respects, position was less carefully thought through. The cumulatively altered structure of social-economic relationships seemed to outgrow its philosophical base. Jeffersonian ideologies were not reformulated as the conditions out of which those ideologies grew were transformed. And so democratic sentiment seemed to lose its philosophical moorings, to become, in a sense, *ideologically rootless;* without a system of thought-out propositions, without long-run objectives, without a consistent base to spring from or a goal to reach—became, in short, both opportunistic and naïve and therefore vulnerable.

So far as the popular elements were concerned, this seeming rootlessness is not difficult to explain at any given point. The fervor of popular resentment against the arbitrary authority of the Old World is easy to understand. So also is the general enthusiasm for the English and the French Enlightenment, and the American and French Revolutions. Liberty, equality, and fraternity were war cries, pulse-quickening slogans. The new and basic truths were "self-evident" and required no proof. And what was "self-evident" to the philosophers was in even less need of proof for the majority of the people. Truth would prevail; the right must triumph; man moved slowly but steadily up the ladder of progress. All the conditions of the frontier preserved the lustiness of his endeavor and strengthened belief in the obviousness of this order of things. Hard work brought results. Camaraderie in the face of odds, and a rough-and-ready code of manners, kept out those who would not play the game according to the rule. Honesty paid; the just were just, and the unjust, unjust. What was right was according to the Bible; evildoers would be punished by an ever-watchful Providence as surely as the sparks fly upward. Every boy carried, not a "marshal's baton in his knapsack," but a statesman's quill or a bookkeeper's ledger in his coat pocket. You could be what you wanted to be, go where you wanted to go, do what you wanted to do. Success crowned all diligence, rewarded all merit. This was the creed of trail and cabin; of bivouac and cracker-barrel.

To put the whole matter somewhat differently, so long as the frontier was the prime carrier of democratic institutions in America, our democracy bore a Jeffersonian stamp. It was rural, agricultural, petty-property-minded, individualistic, self-assertive, independent. The democrat believed profoundly in the slogans of the French Revolution, "Liberty, Equality, and Fraternity," translated to mean, "Every man owns his own home, fears God, votes, and can become a tramp, a bounder, a respected citizen, or a President of the United States at his own choosing." Social philosophies played minor rôles.

Consider, then, the picture of the last half of the nineteenth century and the forces affecting the democratic philosophy. The timing factor was of great importance in the national failure to analyze the deeper meaning of the democratic way of life. Immigration was at a high tide; hordes were drawn from the backward sections of Europe—backward, that is, from the point of view of every significant criterion accepted as progressive in America. The principal carriers of the democratic tradition thus became the native stock, which was too often segregated from the rank and file of the newcomers. This internal separation often promoted, not philosophical awareness of democratic interests, but opportunism.

But the importance of the "melting pot" in the development of the democratic way goes further. One of the greatest "accidents" of cultural evolution caused this most enormous and complicated task of assimilation in all human history to be carried on coincidently with the ascendency of those forms of industrial technique which tend to dissolve the ties of family, of tradition, of common bonds of interest and occupation. What the sociologists call "vicinage" and President Roosevelt more simply terms "neighborliness," were destroyed most quickly for the portion of the population that often was dependent upon the supports of such ties.

Physical mobility—new jobs, autos, buses—increasing with each new discovery and mounting with each passing year, bruised the physical roots of neighborliness and friendliness. Urban life tended to leave people without any sense of home or attachment to locale. New standards of living and new forms of goods broke the old routines centered around eating, sleeping, and recreation. Commercialization transmuted the values of work and leisure, scattered popular forces, undermined the old associations, and supplied no new ones to take their places. "Individualism," in the basest sense, came to dominate popular thinking.

Almost without exception, Americans were property-minded. Certainly property in America had meant something special for the poor who flooded these shores. In the face of boundless natural resources and stimulated by the rise of competitive rules of action in economic activity, the institution of private property meant for the common man not a new agency of oppression but *democratization of the right to have and to hold the essentials of good living*. For the lower orders of mankind this was a revolutionary change in the nature of things. Property was associated and inextricably bound up with the new liberties: ownership of farm, house, livestock; freedom to make contracts to buy what you could afford and sell what you wished; freedom to bargain, to make a gain, to hedge on the future, to speculate on a possible killing. The psychology of the average American citizen was thus adventurous, chance-taking, speculative, imbued with the germinal seed of get-rich-quick. Generally, Americans came to believe in individualism; with their entrepreneurs they suspected government, feared centralization, avoided rules and regulations. They were laissez-faire-minded and property-enthusiastic.

If in the earlier period the common man was *property-conscious* because he identified property-holding with possession of democratic liberties, so in the latter period he became *sales-conscious* because he was led to associate the cumulative outpouring of a widening range of new goods with the thaumaturgic properties of an economic order his ancestors had espoused as the giver of all life to the poor.

For the earlier corner grocery store, substitute the orderly, efficient groceteria. For the germinal factory with its but partially routinized labors and easy freedom between master and men, substitute the vast mechanized plant pouring out goods in endless quantities and coherently regimented cadres working together as with but a single will. For the roll-top desk, the dust, and the careless scatter of papers across the floor at evening time, substitute the spick-and-span office with clean and well-ordered working places, and its serried rows of files. Imagine all this grown by easy steps, but surely and swiftly, from out the chrysalis of the first primitive mass-production plans.

Consider the legend: mass production means more goods; more goods mean larger markets; larger markets require greater emphasis upon ways and means of disposing of the cumulative output. Then, obviously, since mass methods cheapen production and handling, the consuming public must of necessity have lower prices. From the union of science and engineering perpetually spring new products, new sources of creative power, intricate new techniques. Hither and yon and forever on the march, restlessly, ceaselessly, insistently, the secrets are won that man may prosper at the threshold of his knowledge. The potential standard of living must of necessity increase. Obviously, given markets sufficiently large to utilize capacity under competitive conditions, the potential could—nay, inevitably must—be translated into the day-by-day realities of existence.

Thus it came about that a few short decades before the democratic forces in America and the world faced their greatest and most difficult tasks, they were here on this continent drugged with material complacence. To them, like children sporting on some sun-drenched strand unaware of an approaching typhoon, this outlook, this mood, brought with it no realization that disaster was rushing swiftly down the lanes of a pleasant afternoon.

Long before this time, however, even as early as the end of the Civil War, none of the old popular democratic slogans could be made to fit reality. With the decade of the eighties a vast and almost wholly new type of social order had begun its swiftly growing life. And by the time of the World War the course for the future had been set in a new pattern.

The events of the World War, however, and their immediate aftermath, served further to confuse the picture in some respects. But one thing it did make clear. It was no longer possible to escape the conclusion that war touched the interests of the majority of the people. And without far-reaching changes in national systems there could be no prospect of lasting peace. But the fact of greatest significance was that the man on the street in America supported that war because it was to him "war to make the world safe for democracy." Thus, in spite of the materialism of the age, here again was testimony to the moving power of the democratic ideal. Jefferson and Paine had rooted the seed deep. The majority in America, in fact, only too well grounded in a sense of the mutuality of interests which embraces all mankind, stood prepared to sacrifice everything to the end that tyranny and the blind madness of modern wars might forever be dispelled.

This is not mere wishful thinking. One has but to look back over the record to see that such an interpretation is inescapable from the simplest facts of war history. From mountainous evidence it is clear that the vast majority of the American people was unequivocably behind Wilson's Fourteen Points, that it completely approved of the idea of "self-determination of peoples"—the one leading idea which had given rise to our own war of independence—and that it endorsed wholeheartedly every important social tenet underlying the original idea of the League of Nations. The war itself was waged against what was believed to be the capricious use of brutal military power.

Internally, however, democratic elements were considerably confused by a number of changes occurring during the decade of the twenties. What was not easy to see then, and what we can so readily comprehend now, is that much of our post-war prosperity was necessarily temporary in character.

There were many portents which might have given due warning of the major breakdown which was to follow. Technical changes in this period had been throughout primarily of the labor-saving, materials-economizing types. High wages generally brought emphasis upon man-power-displacing machinery. New inventions in the use of chemical processes and the substitution of electric for other forms of energy operated to the same end. The growth of the standards movement, and the perfection of machines and instruments for automatic control added impetus to the displacement of men. Higher boiler efficiencies made of coal a declining industry not in relative but in absolute terms. Farm mechanization began to displace labor with the same ruthlessness which has long been typical of all industrial processes. The spectacular growth of the whole "scientific management" movement streamlined production and distribution methods to the end that fewer and fewer men would be required with each increase in output. Under favorable conditions, all of these technical changes might have meant lower prices and higher standards of living for the whole population. But the historical fact is that they did not.

Meanwhile the entire composition of the democratic elements was being rapidly altered. The depression, like a sudden cold wind, withered the gaudy optimisms of the boom of the twenties. Swept bare of material assurances, the majority of the people began a painful reappraisal of values. With the "New Deal" America began to rewrite the natural-rights philosophy and to think in terms of pushing freedom's frontiers inwardly toward a more realistic concept, to a concept more consistent with life in the twentieth century. Under the leadership of Franklin Delano Roosevelt, the democratic forces of the nation got from economic chaos a rejuvenated belief that the world could be righted, that the evil days were man-made and could be man-remade. America's historic way of life struggled to reassert itself.

At the very time, however, that America took heart at the words, "The only thing we have to fear is fear itself," the Old World fell under new and spectacularly reactionary regimes. Upon the complicated, impersonal rolling of a vast industrial machine, Hitler fitted the old tyrannies of feudalism and promised Germany a world enslaved in return for the slavery of a nation.

In America the very expression "New Deal" was indicative of a mood which asserted that fundamental and far-reaching changes must be made, all of them changes in the direction towards more freedom, towards greater participation of the majority in the affairs of the nation. In Germany Hitler's "I am the state" began the road down which that nation has traveled toward a caste society and the complete removal of any semblance of popular sovereignty.

In the Nazi view the mass of the people, not only of Germany but of the earth, are by biological determination children and fools. They desire only that their creature comforts be taken care of and then that they be harmlessly entertained—so runs the Nazi philosophy; that, in short, they be led. As the Nazis would put it, ". . . the Leader knows the goal and knows the direction. . . . Who carries this spirit in him, who knows the direction, that person is the Leader." Thus, in their view, not the majority but the "elite" should govern and it is but natural that they should. They look upon themselves as the elect of society. They are become the "elite" of the world with the right to dictate, through large spheres of influence, the lives of all human kind.

So far as the society of the world is concerned these aggressors feel themselves beyond all good and evil. And, what is more significant in the development of this view, is the fact that they have set up behavior patterns which promote the rise of rigid class lines that are not limited to their attitude towards labor alone. The rulers of the caste and semi-caste systems of Germany and Japan now aspire to become the governing class of the world. They take the same attitude towards labor, towards investors, customers, the general public, that they take towards humanity as a whole.

The basic democratic soundness of American public opinion in foreign affairs had been considerably sharpened and focused by the course of events in Europe and the Far East. Mussolini's Fascism never enjoyed public approval, from the original triumph in Rome in 1922 down to the present blackmail assault on France. According to every available sounding-board, Japanese aggression in China, Fascist invasion of Spain, Nazi expansion in Europe have been overwhelmingly opposed in the United States.

Months before the attack on Pearl Harbor, America, under the leadership of President Roosevelt, had sensed the nature of the world conflict, and to the man on the street the real issues at stake were understood most clearly in the old slogans of democracy. In newspaper columns, radio addresses, books and articles, this reaching back to the early roots of the nation's philosophy was evidenced in the increasing references to Jefferson, Paine, Sam Adams, Jackson, Lincoln, and Wilson. This is not to say that the continual, internal massing forces on behalf of majority rule have won, hands down, the answer to the question that the depression posed and the New Deal began to answer. The need for a continual restatement of democratic principles is inherent in our social and political organization. But what Pearl Harbor crystallized for America was the realization that modern industrial technology had removed the dikes against Old World tyranny and that the Atlantic and the Pacific—America's Maginot lines—were little more protection than France's steel and cement wall. As the world grew small in time and space the opportunities for tyranny grew large. The issue, then, has become, finally, this: Can the tremendous and deep-rooted hold of the democratic outlook now be mobilized on a worldwide basis and buttressed with the gigantic industrial power of a democratic arsenal? America's answer? "Brethren, ye have been called unto liberty, therefore hold your hold, brethren—pull up well upon the oars, you have a rich cargo, and I hope we shall escape shipwreck—daylight and good piloting will secure all."

# The Definition of the General Will

*JOHN A. CLARK*
*Associate Professor of Philosophy*

## §1

SINCE THE social debacle of the events at the end of the first World War, there has been among Americans a considerable disenchantment with the phrase, "to make the world safe for democracy." As a result, the alternative conception around which we are asked to focus our purpose concerning world affairs today is that of liberty, and more particularly, of certain special liberties which are to be established "everywhere in the world." From the point of view of a search for an adequate philosophy for our national life, doubtless a disillusionment regarding the sufficiency of our points of view and guiding ideas of two or three decades ago is a most desirable thing. But it is questionable whether we gain in clarity of purpose by substituting as our watchword "freedom" for "democracy." Nor is this an unimportant matter. Shall we not ask: On the national and international scene today, what are we working and fighting for? George Santayana has defined a fanatic as "one who redoubles his efforts when he has forgotten his aims." Among all the nations of the world at the present time, the United States bears a peculiar responsibility not to give way to fanaticism.

Surely the concept of liberty is and must remain one of the corner-stones of civilization. But it alone, we need to recall, will not sustain the structure. This fact becomes increasingly plain when we remember the practical meaning which has been taken on by ideals of liberty in the course of recent history. It is a commonplace to point out that, as men have used and rallied around these ideals, they have had, again and again, primarily a negative meaning. Freedom has meant freedom *from* the domination of society by feudal aristocracy, or *from* kingly power, or *from* religious persecution, or *from* bureaucratic governmental control. Characteristic demands of the present are "freedom from fear," and "freedom from want." Such conceptions may tell us what to work, or even to fight, against. And in so far as it is intended that such freedoms are to be established as "liberties," or rights available to all, we know a little, through the idea of freedom, what to strive for. But the negative meaning of the ideal tends to dominate. And that particular form of liberty which represents to any individual or any group a revolt against external controls which at the moment are felt irksome, tends to be *the* meaning of the conception to that party at that time. The place of freedom, and of the various freedoms, in a positive program of social order drops out of the picture. Actually, liberty again and again becomes a watchword of individual irresponsibility, or of the defense of established special interests of one sort or another, which would defy public criticism. It is of small avail that a few scholars and public philosophers constantly warn us against this, so long as they are hesitant to challenge the popularity of the ideal of liberty itself, and so long as they fail to point out to what an extent (if they could really make functional in society their realization of the implications of responsibility in every freedom) the rallying cry of liberty would cease to make the kind of public appeal that now it does make.

Above all, we need in the democracies today a positive vision of the constructive order of life towards which and for which we are to work, making such personal sacrifices as we shall surely be called upon to make. Called upon to fight, we want to know not so much what we are fighting against as what we are fighting for, and to make sure it shall not turn out that we have been fighting, in effect, to perpetuate the irresponsibility, and in that sense the freedom, of any interest in our contemporary social order. To clarify our purpose in this matter, the watchword of freedom is inherently very inadequate. When, in our steadier moments, we seek not so much a banner for our enthusiasms, however important these may be when wisely aroused, but rather a discerning guide and criterion for our public policies, we need to find an inclusive conception of responsible social order, within which, and frankly subject to which, the conceptions of freedom, and of the various freedoms, find their indispensable places.

Such a conception is that of self-government by the people; or popular sovereignty; or government by the general will of the people. It is the purpose of this paper to reconsider the idea of the sovereignty of the general will as central to the understanding of the practical program and public policy of the democratic and freedom-loving nations as they find themselves again at the hour of decision in the tumultuous modern world.

## §2

It is interesting to learn from recent biographical studies that it was no accident of happy phrase, but the result of long practical reflection upon the central meaning of democratic government, that Abraham Lincoln finally succeeded in formulating to his own satisfaction the expression, "government of the people, by the people and for the people." Among the more systematic political theorists, probably the most important single advocate and student of essentially this same conception was Jean Jacques Rousseau. According to Rousseau, the people rule themselves when their general will rules the state, of which, then only, they are truly citizens; and this condition of affairs defines the form of the ideal republic. There are, he tells us, a thousand ways of gathering men together, but only one way of uniting them.[1] And this means the rule of their "general will." To the clarification of the nature of this "social bond" the great Frenchman gave the best efforts of his thought almost throughout the span of his extended career as a writer. It was one of his earliest themes, and one of his last. Obstinately he refused to yield to easy evasions, or to accept as final the facile solutions of the many problems he found surrounding the enterprise on every hand, until many of his outstanding contemporaries, like Diderot, grew impatient and distasteful of his tortuous thinking. It is largely as a result of this fact that we can trace perhaps best of all in the thought of Rousseau some of the various strands of reflection and the search for the solution of various perennial social problems, which weave themselves into a mature, significant conception of popular government.

It is to be remembered, of course, that the term "the general will" was not Rousseau's invention any more than he can claim to have concluded the process of the transformation of its meanings. As has been pointed out by Professor Hendel recently, and by others before him, the conceptions involved find their prototypes at certain points in the thought of Plato and of Aristotle.[2] They are suggested by the practices of the early Roman Republic, and by the views of the Stoic lawyers of the great days of the Roman Empire; and Montesquieu's notion of the "spirit of the laws" is clearly a related one. Apparently the term itself Rousseau learned from Pufendorf, though Diderot was the one who was giving it widest currency among European intellectuals before Rousseau had done so. Later the German, and then the English, idealistic philosophers took up the conception. Among the psychologists, notably Wundt found an important place for it. At the present time perhaps it may be said that the term "the general will" has become unpopular, because of more or less irrelevant metaphysical associations which now tend to attach to it, with the result that there is some danger of losing sight of Rousseau's chief contribution to social philosophy, while his name is remembered mainly, but in a very incomplete and inadequate way, as a source of the romantic movement in European thought. No attempt will be made here, however, to fill in this minimal outline of the history of the conception we are to study. Let us approach it rather simply in the context of certain fundamental and persisting motives which are constantly directive of Rousseau's own thought, and out of which, perhaps, a working definition of the true meaning of the conception of the general will may be seen to emerge.

First of all it is necessary to take recognition of an old conception, taken over by Rousseau, namely, that of the "natural goodness" of man.

Looking out on the European civilization of his day, the young Rousseau was impressed with its empty artificiality, hypocrisy, and gilded brutality and injustice, from which he, as a sensitive, affectionate, careless youth, had been made to suffer severely in a variety of ways; and his early literary reputation was made, of course, by the eloquent, rather disorderly *Discourses,* in which he exposed these evils to the delight, if hardly to the concern, of the sophisticated intellectual society in which he moved. Here doubtless he could not have succeeded so well had he not cast what he had to say into a general pattern which was familiar at the time. We are given a picture of man "in a state of nature" as happy and good, and then told a story of how, with the growth of civilization and the increasing complexity of human associations, simple human goodness is corrupted and made miserable. It is important to remember, however, that always this kind of account of the matter is held explicitly by Rousseau to be largely fictional. He does not claim that there ever was a time when men actually existed in the purity of the "state of nature," but says that for the determination of such historical and anthropological questions he has no basis of sufficient knowledge.[3] The figure of speech of saying that men existed in this state is rather a picturesque and dramatic way of making a point that is only imperfectly expressed through it. The real notion of man's natural goodness involved is rather that of Rousseau's favorite teacher, Plato, for whom such goodness is not so much original in point of time as basic from the point of view of motivation. To such a conception, however, Rousseau does recur constantly, in his later as well as in his earlier writings, so that we may fairly say that it was a fundamental directing faith behind all his thought. Basically man desires and wills what is good, and, conversely, that is good which he wills and desires, except as his purposes are somehow led astray. Accordingly education, rightly conducted, is a process of releasing, stage by stage, the latent goodness of man's mind and heart (so we learn in the late work, *Émile*), and the problem of civil order is maturely stated as that of discovering "a sure and legitimate rule of administration, men being taken as they *are*, and laws as they might be."[4]

In critical reviews of *The Social Contract*, taken as the most important expression of Rousseau's political thought, much stress often has been placed upon the passage in which the ideal "civil state" of man is contrasted with things called natural (as, for example, with man's natural liberty and natural rights), to the distinct disadvantage of the latter; and it may almost be made to appear that in this later treatise the one-time apostle of nature has abandoned his earlier faith altogether. And this much does seem clear from an inclusive survey of his works: that the maturing writer became increasingly aware of the depth of his divergences from the views of many contemporary or near contemporary thinkers who had used the conception of the natural as, in one way or another, a guide to the ideal. Particularly it is true that throughout *The Social Contract* we find forceful criticisms of current conceptions of "natural right," and "natural law." Having pondered Grotius and Hobbes and others in their dealing with this subject, Rousseau turned more and more decisively against many of their basic modes of thought, though these did provide the setting, and much of the natural current meaning, of the terms which he used none too carefully in his early *Discourse*. I submit, however, that in all this there is no justification for supposing that the fundamental principle of *the basic goodness of man's motives* has lost, or in any essential changed, its status in the author's mind, since it does persist so clearly in the *magnum opus*, *Émile*, where the outline of the doctrine of *The Social Contract* is included as an integral part.

So much, then, for the first fundamental, guiding motive in Rousseau's thought. With this he merged a second, no less central for our understanding of the meaning of his political views. That is, he was deeply impressed with the principle that man is what society makes him.

The truth of this general proposition is illustrated in two main ways. In the first place there is the corrupting influence of civilization, and of "the development of the arts and the sciences," upon man. Of this Rousseau frequently retells the story, in a variety of ways, moving rather steadily towards the following central interpretation of the matter. Through his growing dependence upon the unreliable, often unsympathetic, unjust, and brutal forms of social life around him, man is made afraid for himself, and so put on his guard that his native *amour de soi*, or self-respect, which may very well come to include sympathy and respect and love for others, is changed into *amour-propre*, or egoism, seeking power and dominance over others, cherishing the appearance of virtue rather than anything of virtue itself, and devoid of that true human sympathy wherein all the real virtues lie hidden. It is thus that, according to the famous formula, "men are born free, but everywhere they are in chains." But there is also another way in which society may make men what they are, by giving form and maturity of development to their unspoiled *amour de soi*. Social contacts and relations may broaden one's sympathies, enrich his understanding, and give outlet and effective determination of meaning to his native sense of justice. And, we read, "We might, over and above all this, add to what man acquired in the civil state, moral liberty, which alone makes him truly master of himself; for the mere impulse of appetite is slavery, while obedience to a law which we prescribe to ourselves is liberty."[5] The key to the possibility of this constructive line of development might at first seem purely negative. We are told that when fear of men and their institutions does *not* come in, to call out the response of narrow, aggressive, pretentious egoism, and in the absence of such influences, the individual's maturing experiences are allowed to come to him one by one, in due order, then fine social qualities will appear in him progressively, like the unfolding of the flower from the bud. But in the end social life is seen as no less necessary for this than for the alternative, the corruption of human nature. The family, the simple village community, the well-formed state or true "republic," and the "social contract" or voluntary act whereby the individual, in recognition of his relations to the various associations of which he is a part, acknowledges his obligations to society—yes, and even, in due time, for the development of "good taste," a contact with the sophistications of "the arts and the sciences"—all these are shaping conditions without which human nature would remain a matter of mere shifting impulse, and something really hardly human.[6]

Thus, in one way or another, society very largely makes the man; it makes the slave "by nature" a slave, and to the free man it gives his freedom.[7] In this second abiding and guiding conviction behind Rousseau's thinking we find one of his most original contributions. In very recent years a similar point of view has been made the common property of most thinking people. Psychology, psychotherapy, sociology, and economics are among the scientific disciplines which have helped to substantiate the general form, and at many points also the detailed content, of Rousseau's insight; though very often either that insight or some of its direct implications are lost to view, conveniently, in the discussion of social problems. To understand Rousseau we must make some little effort to recognize how constantly and tenaciously his mind clung to this conviction.

We must include, then, among the guiding ideas and convictions which ruled Rousseau's approach to the conception of self-government, these two: the idea of the essential goodness of human nature in point of its motivation; and the conception of the shaping influence of society in everywhere making what they are the actual manifestations of human nature that we see around us. The conception of the general will may be, and, I think, often has been, misunderstood, when it is not seen as an outgrowth, and a further development of the meaning, of these basic principles. We should be prepared to find that for Rousseau the true "social bond"—or the general will—rules in society when the inherently good motives of its members find such joint expression as to establish and maintain the kind of social conditions under which alone such motives may come into their own in effective maturity of development, rather than being thwarted and corrupted. We have to consider, next, what this means, more concretely, in the way of forms of association and of government.

## §3

A figure of speech which appears in *A Discourse on Political Economy*, though it is more picturesque than precise, has its value. Rousseau writes:

> The body politic, taken individually, may be considered as an organized, living body, resembling that of man. The sovereign power represents the head, the laws and customs are the brain, the source of the nerves and seat of the understanding, will and senses, of which the judges and the magistrates are the organs; commerce, industry, and agriculture are the mouth and stomach which prepare the common subsistence; the public income is the blood, which a prudent economy, in performing the function of the heart, causes to distribute through the whole body nutriment and life; the citizens are the body and the members, which make the machine live, move and work; and no part of this machine can be damaged without the painful im-

pression being conveyed at once to the brain, if the animal is in a state of health.

The life of both bodies is the self common to the whole, the reciprocal sensibility and internal correspondence of all the parts. Where this communication ceases, where the formal unity disappears, and the contiguous parts belong to one another only by juxtaposition, the man is dead or the State is dissolved.

The body politic, therefore, is also a moral being possessed of a will; and this general will, which tends always to the preservation and welfare of the whole and of every part, is the source of the laws. . . .[8]

All of this Rousseau calls, "a very common, and in some respects inaccurate, comparison." It is suggestive, however, and corrective of any tendency on our part to take some one or two of Rousseau's later, more careful statements on the same subject, and to suppose that they alone can give an adequate account of the nature of the developed general will of any group, since here the dependence of such a will upon the total organization and organized functioning of the group, considered in all of its aspects, is so clearly stressed. It is important, too, to note that on the same page with the passage just quoted the remark is made that, "Every political society is composed of other smaller societies of different kinds, each of which has its interest and its rules of conduct," and that each of these is to be said to have a general will of its own. It is, then, not only the forms of organization characteristic of political states which can give rise to a "general will." There will be occasion to refer to this point later.

But the account of our subject which appeared in this early work remained vague. Its clarification was undertaken, many years later, in terms of the conception of "the social contract."

It is a most fascinating study to see how Rousseau manipulates this conception to give it a radically different fundamental meaning from that which it had in the thought of the men from whom it was taken over, i.e., primarily from Grotius, Pufendorf, Hobbes, and Locke. Here let us summarize by saying that, in a word, the result is that at the basis of civil society there is an agreement among men as though all alike had said: "Each of us puts his person and all his power in common under the supreme direction of the general will, and, in our corporate capacity, we receive each member as an indivisible part of the whole."[9] And this means "the total alienation of each associate, together with all his rights, to the whole community." The individual then receives back from the community such rights as it may determine as those in which all, equally, are to share. The result, when this has been done, *is* the fully developed general will of the community in question, and its content, or "object," is the law and the current system of justice of the land.

The "contract" so described, however, is not viewed as an historical event. It is an agreement among the members of a community, tacit or explicit, into which they come gradually, by birth in a common land with its common traditions, and through growing mutual understanding.[10] At the same time, the agreement, and its resultant will to a common good is not a mere ideal, but an actuality of mutually considerate convergence of wills, and of adjustments of each towards all the rest. It may be counted on, to be sure, to constitute but one part, and that a small one, of the will of each member of the community, and consequently if the individual's conformity in action to the dictates of the general will is to be assured, it is necessary to set up powers of government which may force him to conform. Yet this means conformity to a part (and, Rousseau would say, the "free" part) of one's own will; and thus it is that we come upon the famous paradox that under the general will, and its system of government, the individual may, and must, be "forced to be free."[11]

But there are ambiguities in this summary account of the matter. We must follow Rousseau more closely, and particularly in the matter of his further statement that the general will of a community must "both come from all and apply to all"; or, as the same proposition is alternatively phrased, the general will must be "general in its object as well as in its essence."[12] Of the two points here, the stipulation that the general will must be "general in its object," has sometimes been taken to be the more fundamental requirement, with the result of quite falsifying, I believe, the whole tenor of Rousseau's thought, and turning it towards a Kantian kind of rationalism which fits in very poorly with the general sense of his other writings, and may be seen, as I shall attempt to show, not to belong to Rousseau at all.

"Every authentic act of the general will," Rousseau says, "binds or favors all the citizens equally." This does not mean that provision cannot be made for special powers which some people, only, can rightfully hold and exercise. For example, there must be magistrates who are granted special powers in enforcing the laws which define and protect any system of rights; and that there shall be such special rights, for a limited class of individuals only, is within the province of the general will to determine. But just what individuals are to have such rights, it may not determine. It must confine itself to decisions of the form that there shall be a class (so far as the general will is concerned, equally open to all), whose members, be they who they may, are to have special rights of a designated sort.[13] Such is the sense in which all decisions of the general will must "apply to all" alike, and its "object must be general," and consist in the formulation of a system of "general conventions." There does seem to be a superficial similarity to the Kantian conception of the moral law, here. But note the reason Rousseau gives for his position. It is that, were the object of the general will not general in the sense stated, then that general will would not "come from all." Rather, favoring certain special individuals, its dictates would in return win the allegiance of these individuals only, and not that of all the rest. Where a decision applies to all alike, however, each will have an equal interest in it, and all may come, wisely, to will that decision in concert.

Now this argument is open to criticism from a logical point of view, while the political conception which it led Rousseau on to introduce—that of the radical separation of the legislative and the executive branches of government—has proved in practice equally untenable. To this topic we shall return very briefly in just a moment. But note, now, the more fundamentally important matter of the form into which the argument is cast. From this two things may be learned.

In the first place, the point that the general will must come from all is clearly taken as more fundamental than the one that it must apply to all. To be sure, the general will is not identical, necessarily, with whatever at any time may be the common "will of all." On this point, implied, indeed, in what has been said above, Rousseau is repeatedly entirely explicit. A demagogue may fool the people, he tells us, until they widely favor something which is not for the common good; a tyrant may terrify them into some sort of unity of action; or one faction within the state may make its particular will prevail; but in such cases "the will of all" is not the general will. It is Rousseau's emphasis on such points that has led to the belief that "generality of object" rather than of "essence," or origin, is really, for him, the defining character of the general will. But in the argument before us the proposition that the general will must be general in its origin is clearly taken as the prior assumption or premise, from which may be derived, as a dependent conclusion, the proposition that the object of the general will must be, in a sense, a general one. Where "the will of all" is not their general will, then, it must be because it does not come from all *in the right manner*. That is, it is an entirely necessary condition, though not a sufficient condition, for the existence of the general will that it should come from all.

And from this point we may go on directly to a second. In the argument we have just traced there is an indication of the *sense in which* the general will of a group comes from all of its members. It, and the system of justice and of common good which it defines, is represented as recommending itself to all *in so far as each sees clearly wherein his own advantage lies.*

The fallacy of the argument affects only the universality of the conclusion that the object of the general will must be general. For it is entirely possible that all may, together, and quite shrewdly, see personal advantage in some entirely particular decision. In fact Rousseau admits this, at a number of points, as, for example, when he asserts that the people may wisely decide that, to meet some special exigency of state, a dictatorship of some particular man shall be established, by common consent, for a specified period of time.[14] Thus it is not possible to deduce unexceptionable "generality" in its object from the requirement that the general will must be general in its "essence" and origin. Rather, the general limitation of the function of the political state to the formulation and protection of "general conventions" must be seen to follow only in so far as other considerations are brought into the picture, such as the constant danger of a corruption of administrators which is inherent in the necessity of granting them special powers whereby to "force men to be free." Thus the proposition that the general will can act only in the establishment of a system of rights, equally open to all, must be seen as applicable only to the general will of that distinctive association known as the political state, and even here only as a rough rule of thumb, to which there are exceptions. But we have seen that there are other institutions, also (perhaps forgotten momentarily in Rousseau's preoccupation with the state) which may have each of its own general will, and, in these, much more particularity of object for their general will may sometimes be possible. Such would seem to be the conclusion to which Rousseau's basic premises truly lead, and his emphasis in *Émile* upon the importance for society of such associations as the family, wherein the nature of social responsibility may first and best be learned, seems to indicate his own mature awareness that the nature of "the social bond" is to be seen also elsewhere, and somewhat differently there, than it is seen in the life of political institutions and the state.

But the principle stands that the general will of any group comes from all the members of that group in the sense of being potentially the will of each, or actually so in so far as each, in recognition of his relation to the group, sees clearly wherein his own advantage lies. That there is, and must be, such a common interest in any group of people who share at all in a common life, and that sound social policy is everywhere to establish the "sovereignty" of such common interests—this may be taken, then, as one simple but foundational thought in Rousseau's doctrine of the general will.

In the understanding of the development of this idea, however, some difficulties remain. In his reinterpretation of the old doctrine of "the social contract," Rousseau holds that the general will of a group is arrived at through mutual adjustments of the nature of mutual understanding and agreements. We have seen that this same common interest can be said to exist in the group only in so far as each sees clearly wherein his own advantage lies. It has a potential existence, only partially actualized. But can there be any real meaning to the notion of a potential agreement? Until it is fully made and understood by all parties to it, is not an agreement just nothing at all?

Phrased in sometimes rather puzzling language, Rousseau has, I think, a rather straightforward answer to this objection, as follows: "All the clauses of the social contract," he says, "properly understood, may be reduced to one." And this clause may be expressed (in terms already once quoted) as the assertion that, "Each of us puts his person and all his power in common under the supreme direction of the general will, and, in our corporate capacity, we receive each member as an indivisible part of the whole." Now the difficulty with this statement is that it may well seem to involve circularity of definition. That is, an understanding of the nature of the general will seems to be presupposed in the statement of the agreement which defines what that will is. This difficulty is avoided, however, if it is observed that there are two closely related meanings which the term may be given, and is given from time to time in Rousseau's writing. In the first place "the general will" may mean, and be so understood by each individual who pledges subservience to it, that complex common purpose, *whatever it may turn out to be,* to which all, under certain conditions of joint deliberation (i.e., in their "corporate capacity" when they "receive each member as an indivisible part of the whole") will come to agree. In the second place, "the general will" may mean the full actual outcome of the joint deliberation in question. Then the general will may exist in a group in the indeterminate form indicated by the first of these two meanings of the term—it may already be their common purpose, created by "the one clause" fundamental to the social contract—though the fuller meaning of the term is not yet determined, and therefore not yet agreed to.

This means that, in the second sense of the term, the general will may be a potentiality only, within the group, while in the first sense it is an actuality. Thus Rousseau tells us that for the full development of a general will many very difficult things are necessary—for example, in the state, the activity of the wise legislator, and the approval of his recommendations by properly constituted assemblies.[15] Yet, pending such developments, "all the qualities of the general will" may be present in the citizens,[16] constituting one part, if in truth only a small part, of the will of each, through the actual common agreement of the fundamental clause of "the social contract"—from which, in due time, many other agreements are to spring.

And the appearance of circularity in the definition of the general will is thus seen to be superficial. The fully developed, concrete, general will of a group is indeed to be defined as that which is the outcome of an agreement to the fundamental clause of the social contract. That is, the general will in the *second sense* stated, is to be defined in terms of a reference to this agreement. And this agreement is, indeed, to be defined through a reference to the general will—but now it is of the general will in the *first sense* that we are speaking, and this is not defined through a reference to any agreement, but rather in terms of certain conditions of joint deliberation out of which agreements issue, when, namely, "in our corporate capacity, we receive each member as an indivisible part of the whole." There is no circularity in this account of the matter.

For its full clarification, however, we require an understanding of the condition of joint deliberation whose outcome is to be the fully developed general will of the group, and here perhaps it must be judged that Rousseau fails us, to a degree, but in a richly suggestive way. To the proposition that all must in their corporate capacity receive each individual as an indivisible part of the whole, we find added the requirement that "all continually will the happiness of each,"[17] and this seems to be presented as an alternative statement of the same principle. It is the basic principle of social equality which has recently been expressed, hardly less vaguely, as the requirement that all be "equally considered." And, in Rousseau, the basis for it seems clearly to be this: Only where the principle of equality is observed can it be certain that the outcome will be a full system of agreements and of common purpose to which each must wish to adhere in so far as he sees clearly wherein his own advantage lies. (In other words, the establishment of conditions of real social equality is the precondition of the development of a true system of liberty, and of responsible "liberties.")

Various special applications of this principle are most interestingly suggested by Rousseau, some of which it may be well to recall in a summary way at this point. Thus, in the state, we are told, it is necessary to prevent the formation of powerful factions or "partial societies"[18]—a principle which many of the New Dealers have recently been questioning in theory, or in practice, or in both, and one to which Rousseau himself elsewhere suggests certain limitations. Again it is necessary that both a love of liberty and a strong "civic impulse" should be very lively forces in a people not hardened into bad customs by bad laws, if there is to be any hope of equal consideration for all in joint deliberations of that people.[19] And the distribution of wealth must be right, so that "no citizen shall ever be wealthy enough to buy another, and none poor enough to be forced to sell himself."[20] Public morality must be simple and sound.[21] Assemblies with universal suffrage should be convened frequently for the purposes of open public debate (though each man must learn to think his "separate thoughts"). In general, the decisions of the majority should be accepted, though the settlement of different types of issues should wait upon different degrees of unanimity, and the presupposition of a trust in the decision of any vote is that "all the qualities of the general will reside in the majority."[22]

But such propositions all have to do with the special problems of the emergence of a general will in a political state; and they need to be varied somewhat to apply to the many varied kinds of state that may be known to history. The universal principle is one of social equality in "corporate" unity such that, to the decisions made under this principle of equality, all are ready to pledge subservience in advance, and to this degree, the general will is present as a fact among the members of the group.

We may summarize, then, as follows: In any organized group of persons their general will is a common interest which is present in each individual in so far as, in recognition of his relationships to the rest, he sees wherein his own advantage lies. It takes on, to a greater or lesser degree, determinate, concrete character through many mutual adjustments and agreements, more or less tacit or explicit, growing out of the basic common understanding that each shall be bound, by force if necessary, to all such further decisions and agreements as are the outcome of joint deliberation when this is so carried on that "all will the happiness of each." In actual human organizations such as, to cite a single example, the European national state, such a common interest and general will does exist in a more or less developed form, as a part, if usually but a small part, of the will of each of its members. The necessary condition for the development of a general will in a group, which may be roughly stated by saying that "all must will the happiness of each," or that all must be equally considered, requires, in general, in the state, that here the general will must confine itself to defining and protecting a system of rights equally open to all, and that in this sense its "object must be general," consisting in the formulation of a body of positive law. Rousseau's own argument, however, indicates that there are exceptions to this principle even in its application to the affairs of the state, and that in the case of other institutions, which may also have a general will, such exceptions may be more numerous.

The discovery within social groups of such a "social bond" constitutes for Rousseau a happy corroboration and further explanation of the principle of the "natural goodness" of man, since in the general will we see how it is that *amour de soi*, and native concern for one's own advantage, may come to include love of others and respect and concern for their happiness. Equally, however, a study of the general will illustrates the principle that men's lives and their guiding attitudes are shaped by the social order in which they live. We see in many ways that only where institutions and forms of social organization are conformable with it, can the general will of a people or a group of any kind develop to any high degree or attain any large measure of control, so that, becoming in its turn the regulating principle of a whole system of social order, it may steadily surround men with the kind of a human environment necessary to an unfolding of the inherent goodness of their natures. And under the persecutions of his later life, Rousseau came to be only increasingly impressed with the rarity and difficulty of the complex social conditions necessary for the rule of the general will.

## §4

We are prepared now to estimate the relevance of this line of thought to contemporary problems.

In the first place, I should emphasize the selective realism of Rousseau's method of approach to his topic. He is not an idealist in the sense of being one who traces out, from certain preëstablished conceptions of what men or society ought to be, a utopian picture of the ideal republic towards which he would have us yearn. His starting ground is human nature and human relations as he finds them to be in fact. Thus not only narrow egotism (with its accompanying tyranny of some man over others) is a fact which experience discovers for descriptive analysis, but also "all the qualities of the general will" among man are facts in a similar sense, marking an inherent trend in human affairs which can be developed by those who will observe the conditions of its development. For the formulation of his social program Rousseau is first and foremost an empirical observer of the nature of social fact. In many parts of our Western World, a long philosophical tradition has encouraged an opposite, and, I think, a largely impotent approach to basic questions of social policy. If the democratic peoples today are not richly to deserve the criticism of their totalitarian contemporaries that the avowed purposes of democracy are inherently ineffective ones, and a cloak for the operation of forces which they conceal without really much deflecting their course of operation, must we not seek to follow Rousseau in this fundamental matter of method in dealing with social questions? To do so at many points would alter our thinking almost past recognition.

In the second place I would note the thorough challenge

to most of what we know as individualism. The rule of the general will of the people involves, we have seen, "the total alienation of each associate, together with all his rights, to the whole community." Only thus, completely governed by the public interest, can a derivative, tentative, but just, apportionment of common rights and liberties, and a true inward freedom—a responsible "moral freedom"—be achieved by the citizen. Every individual is to be respected as he has seldom, if ever, been respected in human history, but *only as* "an indivisible part of the whole." Such is the necessary condition of a "union," and not a mere coming together, of men—the requirement of a way of living together which shall not be full of the seeds of conflict, and of succeeding, unstable tyrannies of the momentarily strong over the momentarily weak. This is not totalitarianism, where the people do not rule, but it is a rejection of any and every individualistic claim to freedom from enforceable responsibility to the public good. Is it, then, an un-American doctrine?

In the third place, however, we must remember at once, here, the limitations of the state as an organ of the general will of its people. This is a principle to the development of which, in accordance with his own fundamental principles, Rousseau never adequately turned his mind. But he clearly laid the foundations for such a development. Sovereignty, or supreme authority, lies with the general will. But only in some of the things which states often attempt to do—namely, in the formulation and enforcement of just laws—can they very frequently claim to exercise such sovereignty; and often, even in the actual body of the so-called laws of the state, the sovereign general will is very little embodied and expressed. In such cases it can and should be sought elsewhere by the true citizen, who, like Rousseau in his later years, may even separate himself from his native state *in order that* he may truly remain the citizen, loyal to and ruled by the general will of men in other contexts of human relationships where its rule does more truly prevail. A wise statesmanship must recognize this principle of the rights of the conscientious objector. It is inherent in Rousseau's thought that the good citizen must be first and foremost a citizen of humanity, and only secondarily a citizen of his country. The conception of the sovereignty of the will of the people is incompatible with the notion of absolute national sovereignties.

And finally a very brief fourth observation: to the theorist, Rousseau presents the problem of a more adequate definition of the basic principle of social equality, since his statements on this score remain important but inadequately clear, while what may be judged most profoundly important in his form of social thought serves to make the understanding of the real nature of equality focal to any comprehension of the social destiny of man.

§5

"A fanatic is one who redoubles his efforts when he has forgotten his aims." In many ways the liberty-loving peoples and nations of the world today are redoubling their efforts. If it is true in something like Rousseau's sense of the words, that "there are a thousand ways of bringing men together, but only one way of uniting them," then only those peoples who make the one way of union their aim and guiding principle of social policy will survive the tests of history. Surely, then, it is time, these days, that we should reëxamine our fundamental social objectives both fearlessly and carefully, not failing to include in our survey some thorough consideration of what is meant by the "sovereignty of the general will of the people."

# Scientific Method & Democratic Procedure

*ELIZABETH DUFFY*
*Professor of Psychology*

SCIENTIFIC method is a procedure for obtaining knowledge. Democratic method is a procedure for determining a course of action. The two methods, though differing in certain respects, show a striking similarity in their fundamental characteristics. Both have developed as attempts to minimize the effects of the essential subjectivity of man's "thinking" and "willing"; both minimize this subjectivity in essentially the same way. The purpose of this paper is to point out the similarity between the two in the problems met and in the solutions arrived at.

The human being, in his quest for knowledge, is confronted by a strange paradox. He himself is the instrument through which knowledge is obtained. His sense organs, his nervous system, his other mechanisms, are the mediating agencies involved in "knowing"; yet knowledge must be purged of the special influence exerted by the nature of the organism, or the individual "knower," if it is to be as adequate as possible for the ends it must serve—if it is, in other words, to represent "truth." The individual cannot know anything except as he receives impressions through his sense organs, elaborates and systematizes these impressions, and later, perhaps, symbolizes and organizes in his thinking the results of many different varieties of impressions obtained in many different situations. The conclusions thus arrived at by the individual will seem to him to represent the "facts" of any given situation or the "truth" about the matter. And yet any conclusion about any matter reached by any individual must inevitably reflect the characteristics of the individual reaching the conclusion. To the extent that the individual's experience has been limited and inadequate the conclusion reached must be limited and inadequate. To the extent that special desires or motivating factors are operating in the individual, the conclusion reached must be distorted by these desires. The knowledge obtained by an individual is *his* knowledge in a very special sense. No one else could have *exactly* that same knowledge, *exactly* that same point of view, for no one else would have had both the same motives and the same experiences as the individual in question.

For an understanding of the essential subjectivity of an individual's knowledge, it is necessary to consider in some detail the psychologist's explanation of the manner in which we obtain our knowledge. The psychologist sees the activity of "knowing," like all other activity, as being derived from the organism's *needs*, or from a condition of disequilibrium which sets the organism into activity which is so directed as to restore equilibrium or satisfy need. It is assumed that, in the absence of need, there would be no activity at all. Our original, or basic, needs are tissue needs—the requirements of the organism for food, for drink, for the release of tensions. As a result of a process of "learning" in a particular social environment (the process of "socialization" of the individual), we acquire other needs, such as the need for prestige, the need to conform to certain ethical standards, the need to satisfy intellectual curiosity. The particular needs which are acquired will depend upon the nature of the society in which the individual develops. Very different needs are reported by ethnologists to characterize individuals developing in different cultures. For example, the need to be "feminine," or to show the behavior expected of a female, will in some cultures lead to the development of a need for aggressive and violent behavior, while in other cultures it will lead to the development of a need for submissive and tender behavior. But, whatever the nature of the need experienced by the individual, that need will set the individual into activity of whatever kind seems most likely to satisfy the need. If hungry, the individual will seek food; if thirsty, he will seek drink; if in need of self-esteem, he will attempt to excuse himself for any behavior which is not in conformity with the standards which he has taken over from society and made his own.

But the attempt to satisfy needs, or to reach goals, requires that the individual interpret the nature of the conditions with which he must deal if he is to arrive at his goal. He must know whether a given object or situation provides a means to his ends or represents an obstacle which must be circumvented. For this purpose he notices this or that. He does not notice *everything*, but only the things which interest him or bear some relation to his goals. Thus even the first stage in the obtaining of knowledge—that of observation—is highly subjective. In other words, what will be observed depends upon the needs or interests of the individual. Observation is subjective in a second sense also; it depends upon the individual's capacities for observation. For example, a child cannot perceive in a situation the same factors which an adult can perceive. This is true not only because his needs are different, but also because his nervous system has not matured sufficiently to enable him to perceive complex relationships, and because his experiences have not been broad enough to provide an adequate basis for interpreting the situation. As the child differs from the adult in what he is capable of perceiving in a situation, so does one adult differ from another in this respect. We can perceive only what we are prepared to perceive. Differences in past experiences, including special training, produce differences in the perceptions or observations of different adults. Moreover, differences in the quality of the structures involved in the perceiving—sense organs, nervous system, etc.—also produce differences in the perceptions of different adults.

Each of us observes, first, what he needs to observe or is interested in observing, and, secondly, what he is able or prepared to observe in the light of his particular equipment of physical structures and his particular past experiences.

In reaching our conclusions about things, or obtaining knowledge, we rely not only upon direct observation but also upon thinking or reasoning. By thinking the psychologist means representing objects and relationships among objects by symbols which stand for those objects and relationships. These symbols are then manipulated, sometimes in "trial-and-error" fashion, until we arrive at a solution to the problem which caused the thinking to take place. For thinking, even more obviously than perceiving, originates in a need or maladjustment of the individual. The direction taken by the thinking is determined by the nature of the need or problem. Thus, the different needs, problems, or interests of different individuals will cause their thinking to follow different lines. And again, as in the case of perceiving, differences in the equipment of different individuals for thinking about a given problem (e.g., differences in physical structures and, especially, in past experiences) will produce differences in the types of conclusion reached. Our thinking is our own *personal* thinking; if *we* were different, *it* would be different.

And yet it is by means of observation and thinking that we attempt to reach objective conclusions, or conclusions independent of the observer—that we attempt to arrive at "truth." And certainly, unless we subscribe to the position of the mystic, there is no more adequate means by which "truth" may be obtained.

In the face of this dilemma, mankind has developed a method by which conclusions may be arrived at which will be somewhat less subjective, which will represent to a lesser degree the personal bias of the thinker. The method is known as scientific method. It involves the pooling of the results of the observation and thinking of many different individuals. Its essential features are in every instance means whereby observations and conclusions are protected, in so far as possible, from the bias, the inevitable subjectivity, of the individual observer. The knowledge which constitutes science is knowledge about which there is more or less agreement. In the absence of agreement, a particular interpretation of events is an hypothesis, not an accepted principle. Hypotheses become established principles only when it can be shown to the satisfaction of other scientists that events do in fact occur as they were supposed by the hypothesis to occur. Science, then, recognizes *degrees of certainty* about the phenomena it describes. Certain phenomena are regarded as facts because their occurrence under certain conditions can be agreed upon by all observers whose training or information makes them competent to judge the situation. Other, often broader, interpretations of the sequence of events, or of the context in which a given event occurs, may, because of the absence of a sufficient number of established facts, command less general agreement. Further investigation of the subject may then establish additional facts which will make untenable some of the interpretations of the phenomena offered. It may indeed happen that all proposed interpretations except one are ruled out and that one then becomes an accepted principle of explanation. Science, then, is a body of knowledge about which there is more or less agreement. This agreement, however, is not accidental. Nor is it secured by external coercion. In fact, science dies where external coercion rather than the inherent logic of events forces agreement. Science, it has often been said, can thrive only in a free society.

Agreement about phenomena is made possible in large part because of the adherence by scientists to that procedure known as scientific method. A scientist attempts to convince a fellow scientist of the existence of a fact, not by appeal to his emotions, not by the argument that personal, racial, or national advantage would be served by accepting what he urges, but rather by inviting his fellow scientist to observe whether under certain carefully described conditions the phenomenon does not indeed occur as he has described it. To this end, that of securing agreement among observers, scientific observations are made under known and, where possible, controlled conditions which can be duplicated by other observers. Frequently, recording instruments are employed in order to make finer observations than human sense organs are capable of or to rule out errors which might be due to characteristics of the individual making the observation. Scientific method, then, aims at objectivity, or the obtaining of knowledge which is not dependent on the special bias or judgment of the individual observer and is, therefore, open to verification by any investigator. It is a method which has, in a sense, made man able to lift himself by his bootstraps. It has made him able in some degree to arrive at "truth" which is not completely dependent upon the "knowing mechanism," or the individual observer by which it is mediated.

It is not surprising, then, that information obtained by this method has proved more useful or has "worked better" in dealing with the phenomena of nature than information obtained by any other means. The insights of poets and philosophers may provide valuable hypotheses, but they cannot be accepted as established facts until they are tested by a technique through which general agreement may be obtained; for these insights, though they may be the insights of very superior human beings, are still insights of *individuals* and are subject, therefore, to all the special influences which have molded the individual. They are subject to his individual desires and prejudices, to the limitations of his individual experience, to his special capacities and incapacities.

This inevitable bias, or subjectivity, in the opinions and desires of individuals has presented mankind with a problem, not only in acquiring knowledge, but also in determining the course of action of social groups. If social cohesion is to be maintained, and thus the greatest ultimate satisfaction of the needs of all is to be secured, a common course of action must be followed by the members of social groups. But how is this course of action to be determined? The desires, the opinions, of one individual will be different from those of another—and necessarily so. Individual determination of the course of action, except within certain well-defined limits, would, therefore, result in the disruption of society. Shall the course of action, then, be decided by a leader, or dictator, who is presumed to have greater wisdom than the other members of the group? This solution offers the difficulty that any dictator or leader is still an individual, with the particular bias in aims, values, opinions, which any individual must of necessity have as a result of his individual experiences. No individual can plan adequately for a group, because no individual can possibly contain within himself, or even be sympathetic toward, the diversity of aims and opinions found among the members of the group. A benevolent despot could be benevolent only toward aims which he himself could understand. The course of action which he would decree would represent only very partially the desires and needs of the group. Is it possible, then, to obtain any more complete representation of individual desires and at the same time maintain social cohesion? This question is, basically, very like the question which we asked earlier, namely: Is it possible for the individual "knower" to arrive at knowledge which is not merely his own particular point of view but is, rather, an interpretation which can be accepted by the group as a whole? The answer to the second question proves to be not unlike the answer to the first.

Mankind has developed, as a means of determining the action of social groups, a *method* which to some degree circumvents the subjectivity of the individual and yet gives representation to individual desires and interests. It is the method of democratic procedure—or the determination of a course of action, not by an individual, but by the pooled judgments of all members of the group. A course of action thus decided upon will represent, not the special interests or desires of a few individuals, but rather the desires of a majority of the members of the group. Hence, adherence to this course of action can be obtained with a minimum of coercion. Group unity is attained, not by the imposition upon all of the necessarily partial and subjective point of view of one or a few, but by the choice of that course of action which emerges as most representative of the common features in the diverse and often conflicting aims of the members of the group.

To pursue this method of determining action is difficult. Care must be taken that certain members of the group do not, through special forms of coercion, such as the use of wealth or the superior organization of active and determined minorities, control the expression of the will of other members of the group or control the policy of the group in defiance of the expressed will of the majority. Moreover, individuals who are not in agreement with the majority of the group will need protection from coercion by the group in those areas where it is not essential that unity of action be maintained. The aim of democratic procedure is to maintain the unity of the group and at the same time to give the widest possible representation to the great diversity of needs and opinions which are necessarily found where we have large numbers of individuals, each with different potentialities and each developing under different conditions. In other words, democracy is a method developed to resolve the dilemma produced by the fact that man desires, perceives, and thinks as an *individual* but must often act as a member of a *group*.

Like scientific method, democracy attempts to solve a problem created by the essential subjectivity of man's responses. Like scientific method, it relies upon the correction of one opinion by another, upon the emergence of some degree of agreement from the pooling of many individual opinions. Science has defined more specifically than democracy a means whereby agreement of individuals can be obtained. Scientific issues are not settled by mere majority vote, even of scientists. They are settled rather by recourse to a method of observation which involves so many checks and precautions, so much guarding against subjectivity, that observers employing this method may in many instances reach complete agreement upon a given phenomenon. In the absence of this agreement the phenomenon in question is not regarded as a scientific fact. In determining the course of action of a social group it usually is not feasible to delay the decision until suitable tests of "facts" can be made and complete agreement on some points arrived at. Moreover, the choice of a course of action often involves either choosing between, or arriving at a compromise of, conflicting interests of individuals or groups. Hence majority vote, rather than complete agreement, must usually be the basis for the decision. However, if it were possible in a democracy to see that each voter was as well *informed* about the facts in a situation as each scientist is informed about the facts pertaining to a given point of issue, it is possible that a greater degree of agreement in political affairs could be obtained. Unlike democracy, science prescribes for its observers a certain training, certain information, certain ways of getting new information. But it must also be recognized that the issues about which the scientist is able to obtain agreement are usually issues of less vital and immediate concern to most men than are the issues upon which agreement is sought by means of democratic procedure. The closer the relationship a given "fact" bears to the conflicting strong desires of men the more difficult it is to gain assent to that fact, the more motivation there is for disagreement.

Rationalization, or thinking in accordance with one's desires, is characteristic of man. Indeed, it is doubtful whether any one of us is capable of doing anything else. All human activity, including thinking, has its origin in a need of the individual and represents an attempt to satisfy that need. Thus it is to be expected that man should arrive at conclusions or beliefs which are *satisfying* to him. It is the task of the psychologist to explain, not why man's conclusions are subjective, but, rather, why they are to any degree objective. The explanation usually given is that they are as objective as they *have to be*, and no more so. Some degree of objectivity is necessary if man is to cope successfully with his environment; and, since all behavior is aimed at adjustment, behavior which results in maladjustment tends to be eliminated. For example, it may please a child to interpret a candle flame as an attractive object into which to stick his finger; but, if he acts on this interpretation, which takes account merely of his desires and not of the objective nature of the situation, his finger is burned. His interpretation is modified by the "check-up by results." In this way our interpretations of the world around us are forced to take into account what might be called "objective reality." However, we resist modifications of interpretations which are in line with strong motives, and, where there is no adequate "check-up by results," we persist in interpretations which are close to the heart's desire. For example, we picture a future life of whatever kind may appeal to us and, in the absence of any unexpected and undesired consequences following upon this belief, we hold to it without question.

But in dealing with the material environment and with his fellow men, man has learned, to some degree, that he must take account of the nature of things from points of view other than those of his own desires. He must do so for the reason that, if he does not, his desires will be thwarted, his needs will fail of satisfaction. Confronted with the necessity of attaining some degree of objectivity in his thinking and of considering to some extent the course of action desired by others, he has developed certain procedures which are of aid in achieving these ends. To assist him in attaining objectivity in his thinking, he has developed scientific method, which attempts to eliminate the observer from the observation and the thinker from the conclusion reached. To assist him in determining the course of action of social groups, he has developed democratic procedure, which attempts to arrive at the "general will" rather than the desires of an individual or a limited group of individuals. Though differing in details, these two methods have in common the attempt to arrive at conclusions which are not dependent on the special bias or judgment of an individual—the attempt to circumvent the essential subjectivity of human thinking.

# Psychology, Social Science, & Democracy

*WILTON P. CHASE*
*Assistant Professor of Psychology*

"All men are created free and equal." This is the basic democratic American faith. It is toward putting this faith into action that our energies to some extent have been bent for the past hundred and seventy-five years. The social sciences have developed rapidly during the past fifty years with the aim of better implementing and speeding the attainment of the American ideal. Of these social sciences, history views the current human endeavors in the light of the past record of men struggling toward similar goals; sociology studies the effectiveness of the organization of men into various collective enterprises for the satisfaction of their needs; economics is interested in the amount and use of our material wealth which we employ in our constant struggle for more and more adequate adjustment; political science surveys the effectiveness of our political structure as an instrument in a democracy for guaranteeing the "life, liberty, and pursuit of happiness" of the individual. But since all these social sciences deal with individuals as they group themselves into the various identifiable social patterns, the basic science of them all is psychology, by reason of its scientific study of the individual. Taken together, then, with psychological foundation, the social sciences constitute a functional area of increasing knowledge, which promises eventually to lead men closer and closer to the realization of their fondest hopes and ambitions.

Psychology approaches its study of the effectiveness of the social order from two angles. First, it is concerned with the basic needs of the individual which he must satisfy in order to live as a reasonably well-adjusted organism and to procreate his kind. Secondly, it must always be critical of the social arrangements through which the individual is expected to satisfy these needs. In the first instance it must enter into social planning to help insure adequate means for the satisfaction of the individual's basic needs. In the second instance it must continually evaluate the effects of society upon the individual. Unless the efforts of the psychologist and the social scientist are to be sterile and academic, and, therefore, unproductive, they must work together in close harmony to insure responsible action.

There is no doubt among the leading social philosophers of this country that the democratic way of life is in the long run the most intelligent and satisfying way of life for individuals who must perforce live together. The philosophy upon which it is based is a workable one. It is pragmatic. It provides for change when change is needed. It does not perpetuate absolute ideals of tradition. It is interested in the welfare of the individual first and last. It does not support the idea of some hypothetical and non-existent "state" above and beyond the reach of the individual. It depends upon growth and development of its individuals for its own perpetuation. It does not attempt to impose a way of life ready-made upon the individual for him to accept without question. It assumes that each new generation must learn the democratic way of living for itself with the resultant profit from the progress that only eternal youth can make. Historically, democracy has existed because of the belief of the people in a way of life for themselves. It does not assume that an individual is born to an inevitable social order. It assumes respect for the individual personality as over against complete subjugation of individuality to a leader. It expects (though it has not yet fully attained) social reciprocity among individuals and nations of individuals instead of having the strong individual or nation dominate the weak. It demands intelligent thinking on the part of the individual as his contribution to the progress of the government which represents him. It deplores the emotionalism of blind faith and attachment to the thinking of leaders. The appeal to reasoning and pragmatic reckoning is the *sine qua non* of democracy. It assumes that the individual will be self-reliant and responsible in carrying out his obligations. It abhors compulsion, using it only when the individual fails to meet his obligations. Above all, it furnishes the only climate in which an individual may discover for himself his unique talents and develop them for the mutual satisfaction of himself and others.

This brief statement merely sketches some of the focal points in the frame of reference in which the psychologist and the social scientist must work in a democracy. And they have a peculiar obligation to apply their scientific findings with the ends of democracy in view, for scientific method demands freedom of investigation for arriving at independent and objective conclusions on the basis of discoverable fact alone. Democracy alone has provided for this freedom. The scientist, especially perhaps the psychologist, thus has a clear obligation. He must discover ways and means to promote the continued growth and development of a democracy in the interest of the corresponding growth and development of its individuals. The freedom for investigation which he enjoys in a democracy has enabled him to build science on a firm foundation of truth. Unless he strives continually for the better realization of democracy through the more adequate employment of that truth in the interest of all and not of the few, he is merely fiddling while Rome burns.

In employing psychology to help achieve the democratic way of life, the social scientist has a wealth of fundamental facts concerning human behavior upon which to draw. These facts deserve more employment than they have so far received. If the engineer overlooked the fundamental facts of physics and chemistry, his achievements would not be what they are. There was a recent example of this in the collapse of a large bridge, in the planning of which the engineer had failed to take into account the wind resistance of the structure. A few openings would have lowered this resistance, and the bridge would still be standing. When we go to a physician, we expect him to employ his knowledge of physiology in diagnosis and treatment. The failure of medical quacks and charlatans because of their failure to apply the knowledge of physiology helps to increase the population of cemeteries. Psychology is in the same relation to social science. Institutions, societies, governments, international relationships disintegrate through lack of use of fundamental knowledge of psychology. The psychologist, of course, has no perfect understanding of human personality. Neither has the doctor a perfect knowledge of physiology, or we should not continue to have common colds and cancer as frequently as we do. The lack of perfect understanding should not stand in the way of applying what we do know. Perfect knowledge is an ever-vanishing mirage. It is a question of relative efficiency. If we can increase the percentage of success in any endeavor by the use of what scientific knowledge we have, its employment is justified. In any case, the practice of successful social science must draw upon the scientific knowledge of human behavior as gleaned by the psychologist.

What has the psychologist discovered about human behavior which is of fundamental value to the social scientist? He knows, first of all, what are the basic biological drives which must be satisfied in order to maintain the minimum of effective adjustment. He understands the learning process by which individuals modify their behavior. He has revealed the function of emotions for adjustive behavior. He measures the individual differences, general and specific, among the various abilities of man. He understands attitudes, beliefs, values, prejudices, and ideals. He has analyzed the nature of morale. Work, efficiency, and fatigue are subject to his analysis. Above all, he comprehends the integration of personality, which is all-important for maintaining nervous and mental balance in the face of difficulties. These are a few of the fundamental areas of information in which the psychologist's knowledge, though incomplete, furnishes a basis for a workable applied social science.

What are the social needs for which the psychologist must help guide the individual in his development? These needs fall roughly into four overlapping areas. They are vocational, social and economic, home and family, and personal problems. Contrary to biological needs, the needs in these areas are shifting and fluid as conditions change in the social relationships of man. At all times they must be evaluated in terms of how well they integrate with the biological needs. The history of society is the record of strivings of men attempting to discover better and better organized social means of obtaining satisfaction for their basic needs.

Here is where we must briefly take into consideration the contributions of the physical and biological sciences. They have equipped us with more adequate tools for living. How adequately individuals have employed them is again the problem of the social scientist. The psychologist views the products of his brother scientists as providing the individual with more and more intelligent solutions to his problems of adjustment growing out of his biological and social needs. He realizes that not all men are able to employ them usefully to improve the general welfare. He further knows that not all men even want to employ them intelligently to the benefit of all. Here again we must return to the fact that we assume that our democratic philosophy is to be the governor of men's motives if it is to be truly operative. It must find its expression in responsible action, not alone in ideals and beliefs. Science furnishes the information for arriving more intelligently at responsible action. In fact, since the discoveries of science are the result of the work of our most able men, for the average man it extends his intelligence. It can be truly said that through science civilization has outdistanced evolution. Herein lies the great challenge for the social scientist. In the face of this, how can our social organization be made effective to insure for the individual his continued equality of opportunity, freedom of thought and action, and rights, privileges, and duties of a free man? The progress of scientific discovery and invention makes for inevitable specialization of human effort. It affects all fields of endeavor: agriculture, industry, education, distribution, finance, homemaking, and even science itself. Only philosophy can supply the unifying principles to hold the separate specialists together for a common purpose. The problem of instilling our philosophy is that of education, through the home, the school, the playground, and the church. Only through the development of an intelligent philosophy can we expect that our scientific achievements will be employed to the ends of our democratic ideals. The average man in a democracy must have a solid democratic character to employ what he does not always understand in the interest of maintaining the "greatest good to the greatest number." This is especially true in a democracy where the average man more often than not finds himself in the position of power and influence, trusted and respected by his fellow men, who placed him there by way of the democratic rule of the majority. It is the great and everlasting responsibility of those who are charged with the education of each new generation. If they fail, democracy fails.

In the practice of social science, psychology should become the linchpin to hold it to the democratic philosophy. The psychologist is the only scientist who studies the human personality in all its ramifications, its development, needs, and integration. He faces the problem of adjusting the individual to the demands of living, on the one hand, and of helping to guide the development of social institutions, better to fit the needs of the individual, on the other hand. In giving such help, he improves the individual's democratic freedom of choice. Personal and social maladjustments hamper the individual's chances for happiness and the free exercise of his potentialities. Every step taken, therefore, in the interest of eliminating maladjustment aids in removing restrictions upon the individual's freedom of action.

From the standpoint of helping the individual to select his field of special effort, it is the psychologist's job to discover as accurately as possible what each individual's special talents are. In a democratic society it must be assumed that each individual must prove his worth through contributing in some capacity to the group effort. The psychologist is concerned with helping each individual to select that effort, whatever it may be. It must be in the area where the individual will demonstrate the most efficiency, industriousness, interest, and, above all, ability. Careful selection on the part of the individual is the first step in his realizing his greatest achievement and contribution to the welfare of himself and his fellows. Lacking any or all of the outcomes in personality which are deemed desirable for successful adjustment, the individual becomes in some degree a liability to society rather than an asset. The psychologist visualizes no Utopia, but he does foresee a decrease in the number of misfits who become the dregs of society. It is not beyond the realm of possibility to say that he already has within his grasp sufficient knowledge to produce a significant reduction in the incidence of mental disorder, feeble-mindedness, and criminality, if full employment were made of his knowledge by the psychiatrist, educator, personnel manager, and the social scientist. To refer to one recent experiment conducted jointly by the psychiatrist and the psychologically-minded educator, one group of school children was given psychiatric care and treatment, while another group was held as a control group with no such attention. Over a six-year period the group receiving psychiatric attention showed a significant decrease in the problems of adjustment, while the control group showed an equally significant increase in such problems.

One of the most significant gains which psychology has

been able to achieve has been in the field of educational practice. It has taught the teacher to give his first attention to the growth and development of children and youth. It has shown that subject matter is merely a means to that development, not an end in itself. In all educational programs which consciously take into account what is known about the development of the personality, the students—elementary, secondary, and collegiate—excel in their progress as measured in terms of the development of the total personality over those who have been in the traditionally subject-matter-minded schools. What is more, they do exactly as well in subject-matter achievement as measured by objective tests. The psychologist's progress in guiding education has been notable, because most psychologists are within the educational framework where they have had a better chance to influence thought and, more important, practice. In those schools where notable progress is being made, the guidance program, managed by people well trained in psychology, is the key to the successes being achieved. Equally notable, but more local, successes can be pointed out in industry, where psychology, functioning through the personnel manager and the industrial psychologist, has been able to reduce fatigue, accidents, spoilage, labor turnover and lost time with corollary increases in the earning power, personal satisfaction, health, industrial morale, efficiency, and industrial output per man-hour. This has been accomplished through more scientific selection and placement of workers—evaluating their health, talents, and temperament, largely by actual tests and measurements—and through studying and improving the actual working conditions.

The scientific adjustment of the individual to the society in which he must live has only just begun. It has proceeded far enough to demonstrate that through the employment of the skill and knowledge of the psychologist, the personality of the individual can be more and more successfully and happily adjusted. Every increase in the percentage of successes in adjusting individual personalities means a corresponding increase for the individual in the degree of self-reliance, sense of personal worth, feeling of freedom, and sense of belonging in the social milieu. It means a corresponding decrease in maladjustment, physical, mental, and social. It means more happiness and contentment with the social order as against unhappiness and discontent.

Psychology, however, would miss its social obligation if it tried to serve the individual merely in a palliative capacity. In fact, in such a capacity only, it would be doomed to failure. It has a clear duty to help direct the efforts of the social scientist into channels which will better furnish the individual with more effective social organization for obtaining the satisfaction of his needs. All fields of investigation seem clearly to have a triple obligation: to amass knowledge, to develop appreciation of values, and to initiate responsible action. Through fulfilling these obligations to the best of their ability the social sciences and psychology can serve, in mutually interdependent capacities, to promote the common welfare of the individual through progressive improvement of the social order. In order to achieve these goals in an effective manner they must pull together, because in unity there is strength. In working separately they fail to achieve mutual understanding and respect. Their separate efforts are all too likely to give the impression of division of purpose. To the uninformed, the enemy of enlightened social effort can play up this disunity as a sign of weakness, as indeed it is. The social sciences have failed to arouse the popular imagination because of their petty bickering and apparent diversity of purposes. As long as this condition exists, faith in their capacity to initiate responsible action will be lacking, regardless of how much knowledge they possess and how keen is their appreciation of the values to be achieved in the social order. Failing in their duty to become more functionally valuable than they are at present, they will continue to occupy an almost purely academic position. From all indications, a purely academic contribution will not much longer be accepted as a justifiable excuse for existence.

It is not for the psychologist alone to say in what way he can contribute to the common effort of the social scientists. It is clearly a problem for coöperative effort. The psychologist is the expert for studying the nature of the individual. He is ready for the social scientists to employ him in their efforts. His position is one of serving them. Here again the analogy of physiology in its relation to medical science is an illustration of the specific relationship which could exist. The physiologist studies the organic functions of the body. The medical scientist employs the physiologist's knowledge and turns to him for help in the solution of problems which are encountered in the practice of medicine. If the physician wishes to employ a certain drug, he first checks all possible physiological reactions to it. If the social scientist, working, probably, under a governmental mandate, should wish to try a new social organization, he likewise could turn to the psychologist for a check upon all the psychological effects which can be discovered. If the physician employs a drug which helps in only a small percentage of cases and hinders in a large percentage, he is soon apprised of that fact. If the application of certain social precepts improves the lot of a small percentage of the people affected and injures the chances for adjustment for a large percentage, the social scientist likewise should be informed of that fact. The psychologist has at his command many instruments for measuring the degree of adjustment in individuals. He is obtaining more and more effective ones all the time. He, in turn, employs the statistician to aid him in his analyses of these instruments and what they measure. To point to but one example, the polls of public opinion carried by nearly every newspaper in this country are the direct outgrowth of the efforts of the psychologist and the statistician working in close harmony. The polls as now employed are crude; yet their accuracy in gauging reaction has been demonstrated in terms of actual results, as in presidential elections. There are even better techniques known to the psychologist which await employment by the social scientist on much larger scales than they have been employed to date. A few examples are attitude scales, market surveys, and personnel methods. Their more widespread employment awaits a closer coöperative effort among all concerned with the social well-being.

The psychologist's function in the democratic process seems clear. He can serve to help implement the democratic dictum that all men are "created free and equal." He knows that they are not free and equal if it is a question of the talents which they possess. They are, however, or should be, free and equal in the opportunities for developing those talents which they do possess in order to contribute to the common effort for building a society of self-reliant men. No matter what the task, no matter what the talent that the task demands, there are men to fit it if it falls within the range of human capacities. The psychologist's job is to help the individual discover as accurately as possible the degree of his talent. It is his duty to attempt to awaken all to the value of each individual's talents, no matter what they may be. Unless the democratic order provides for the realization by each individual of that which he can do best, with adequate return for his efforts, there will be unrest and disaffection. The seeds of revolution lie in the unfulfilled needs of men. The seeds of evolution lie in the progressive realization of more and more adequate adjustment through meeting the needs of all men in more satisfactory ways. We make progress in the evolution of a democratic order when adequate opportunities, compensation, and protection are afforded for the development of each individual personality. As we increase the percentage of successful adjustments among men, we increase the degree of success of the social order. The challenge to democracy is clear. If it protects and encourages the development of the individual, utilizing him effectively, both from his and society's standpoint, it will survive as a way of life. If it fails in this objective for a large majority, there will exist the basis for trying a different social order, even if it is promoted only by a minority group in the beginning. It is a significant challenge in turn to the psychologist and the social scientist to join forces to help guide, in as intelligent a manner as possible, the growth of the democratic way of living. We in America still accept democracy as the best prescription for effective social living yet devised in the history of civilization.

# Napoleon & Hitler: New Order & Grand Design

*EUGENE E. PFAFF*
*Associate Professor of History*

*In this titanic struggle between the present and the past, I was the arbiter and the mediator; I sought to be the supreme judge, all my government and all my diplomacy being directed toward this goal.*—Napoleon.[1]

THE SIMILARITIES between dictators strike us at once. Indeed, resemblance is inevitable. The rule of such men always involves ruthlessness, brutality, savage efficiency—the same everywhere and in all periods of history. There are, however, a number of similarities between Napoleon and Hitler which are beyond the ordinary.

Both are known in the popular mind as men of humble origin, "little corporals."* After serving terms in prison, charged with treason, both of these militaristic nationalists set forth on careers which they fondly imagined resembled those of Caesar and Alexander the Great. The lives of both illustrate the adroit use of histrionics. In each case there was an early frustration of artistic aspirations. Napoleon wanted to be a poet and litterateur; Hitler still dreams of returning to his painting. Both careers show what happens when a neurotic ascends to power. The vagrant lock of hair, the affected stance, the extraordinary walk—these physical features are remarkably similar. The rise to power of both Napoleon and Hitler was financed by syndicates of capitalists; and in both instances this relationship with the upper bourgeoisie was a closely guarded secret. Napoleon always spoke bad French; Hitler is far from a master of German. Both were outsiders, parvenus who came to countries which they later dominated.

* Napoleon was never a corporal; his military career began with the rank of second lieutenant. The phrase "little corporal" was used by his troops as an expression of devotion.

Both came from southern lands to northern capitals which exercised a peculiar fascination for them. Napoleon was always something more than a Frenchman, and Hitler has been aptly described as "the no-more-Austrian and never-quite-German." Each dictator made use of bourgeois fears: Napoleon played upon the menace of Jacobinism, Hitler upon the threat of Communism. Both mastered western Europe, only to run head-on against the stubborn English refusal to permit the existence of a continental empire. Frustrated on the Channel, each turned to the invasion of Russia. In both cases, the invasion of Russia was preceded by an alliance with that country. Neither alliance was more than paper—a fact understood by both Napoleon and Alexander in 1807 and by both Hitler and Stalin in 1939.

Both Napoleon and Hitler turned social revolutions into drives for conquest. Both regarded, or at least affected to regard, themselves as "men of destiny," whose task it was to set up a new order. Both found "fifth columns" of sympathizers in the countries which they attacked. Both made masterly use of propaganda, Napoleon in seizing power and in paving the way for another Bonaparte to ascend the throne of France, Hitler in sabotaging his enemies and in converting the German people to his creed. Both conquerors were adept in using the "psychology of terror."

Both Napoleon and Hitler were interested in history; both were profoundly moved by it. Witness Napoleon's comment: "May my son often study history and reflect on it, for it is the only true philosophy."[2] Moreover, it is rather evident that Hitler has been influenced by Napoleon's career. Witness Hitler's trip to the tomb of the Corsican when Paris fell; recall also the German suggestion that the ashes of Napoleon II be taken from Vienna to Paris. Some other facts are worthy of notice: in 1914 the German press was loud in its praise of Napoleon as the creator of the Continental Blockade and as the author of the plan for uniting Europe against England; in 1922, when the Fascists assumed power in Italy, the study of Napoleon was made a compulsory course of history instruction.

Like Napoleon, Hitler is a militarist. But Napoleon was well educated in a military sense, whereas Hitler knows little of the art of warfare. The military success of both conquerors was due to the technical superiority and the bold tactical methods of their armies. Their victories were in large part the result of the mediocrity of the opposing forces. Both were reckless gamblers, risking countless lives in bold offensives. This fact gave them superiority over their more cautious enemies. Both used the ruthlessness of total war. Both wanted victories for direct political benefits. They were out to crush the enemy, impose their wills upon him, keep him in subjection.[3]

But the differences between these would-be masters of the world are fundamental. As Philip Guedalla has said: "Historical parallels, even since Einstein, rarely meet."[4] Perhaps most important of all are the differences in the circumstances which produced these dictators. Both rose to power in chaotic periods in which the insistent demand was for order and security. Yet Napoleon inherited a revolutionary tradition which limited what he might do in the way of innovation. No dictator could undo the fundamental socio-economic changes engendered by the French Revolution. The coming to power of Hitler, on the other hand, was the beginning rather than the end of a revolution.

Contrary to a commonly accepted idea of temperament, the Latin dictator was the one who possessed a cool, penetrating intelligence and a tremendous amount of self-control. His German counterpart is the emotional fanatic. Napoleon was very much the ordinary man in his fondness for the daily bottle of Chambertin and in his numerous affairs with women. This is in singular contrast with the vegetarian, teetotaling totalitarian from Austria. The Corsican's interest in the intellectual and the rational differs markedly from the romanticism, the anti-rationalism, and the anti-intellectualism of Hitler.

Despite Napoleon's overweening ambition, the primary result of his conquests was the extension of the principles of the French Revolution. The ideals of liberty and equality were violated by the Corsican, but nonetheless they were implanted firmly among the peoples whom he conquered, indeed even among those whom he failed to conquer. The Napoleonic empire served as a stimulus to the development of both modern nationalism and modern democracy. No one can well accuse Hitler of spreading the principles of the French Revolution. In fact, the whole Nazi movement stems from the revolt against the ideas of the French Revolution.

The Napoleonic plan for world domination was the Grand Design; the Hitlerian dream is the New Order. Neither policy is any too clearly delineated. Napoleon was too much the man of action to set down in writing any appreciable amount of his plan. Moreover, it is evident that Napoleon was an opportunist, that his ambitions grew with his victories. The Nazis, anxious to avoid the creation of an anti-German alliance by the rest of the world, have followed a policy of deliberate deception as to their goal. Hitler himself has never given the official version of the New Order. Yet enough is known in each case to permit a comparison that is enlightening. The method of comparison used will be an analysis of both the New Order and the Grand Design in the light of their respective policies: economic, political, social, religious, and racial.

The New Order is widely advertised as a plan to create a united Europe. More to the point is a statement by the Nazi Minister of Economics, Walther Funk, that the New Order is designed to give the Reich maximum security and the German people maximum consumption of goods. To achieve this, all Europe is to become an economic unit. Complete autarchy is not the goal, but all trade with the rest of the world is to be handled by Germany. Europe is to be self-supporting in the essentials. The foreign trade of Europe, organized into a single bloc, will give the Reich tremendous bargaining power in the markets of the world. Germany makes it clear that she will not allow Europe to trade with the other states of the world except as isolated units; no rival trade combinations will be tolerated. Continuous employment is to be maintained by state investment in public works.[5]

Germany is to be the industrial center of this new Europe, with the highly industrialized areas of near-by countries annexed to the Reich. The remainder of Europe is to form a great agricultural and raw material hinterland. With industrial power concentrated in Germany, there can be no military strength elsewhere in Europe. The large German market is guaranteed to the agrarian hinterland by long-term contract. But in return for its products the agrarian area will get inferior goods at rather high prices. The people of the vassal states are to be exploited—the usual procedure in colonial imperialism. Private property will continue to exist, but its rights will be so sharply limited that one can hardly call the system capitalistic. The economic system will operate to benefit the state rather than to produce profits. A government bureaucracy will determine what is to be done rather than a capitalistic class of owners. Economics will be reduced to what Hitler believes is its proper sphere—subordination to politics.

Napoleon's economic plan for Europe and the world was by no means so comprehensive as the New Order. He assigned to France commercial and industrial hegemony in Europe, and he was confident that Europe would dominate the world. But he was, quite naturally, unaware of the increasing importance industry was to assume in life. Napoleon lived in an agrarian and mercantile era. Obviously his design for empire would be quite different from that of Hitler, a man living in an industrialized land and in the midst of a technical civilization.

Napoleon's Continental System was directed, like the New Order, at destroying England as an industrial and commercial power. France was to take over the dominant position of England. Unable to reach England with his army, Napoleon sought to destroy her trade with a self-blockade of the whole European continent. This Continental System was an example of mercantilism, of government regulation of commerce in minute detail, of economic policy used for political ends. Napoleon's adoption of such a policy can be explained, in part, by his desire to preserve France's store of hard money. The Corsican had learned to hate and fear the dangers of a paper currency as a result of the experiences of revolutionary France with depreciation and national bankruptcy. Another aspect of his Continental System was a scheme to dump French industrial products on the satellite states of Europe. In its latter stages, Napoleon turned the System into a gigantic device for collecting revenue.

Despite Napoleon's Continental System, there was nothing in his regime comparable to the economic totalitarianism of the Nazis. Capitalism was comparatively "free" under the Corsican. Indeed, the development of laissez-faire capitalism was one of the principal results of the French Revolution. Napoleon was forced to perpetuate it. His ascent to power hinged so completely upon his aversion to economic feudalism that it would not be too inaccurate to call him a "bourgeois dictator."

Napoleon, like Hitler, approached economics with political motives. He was hostile to a policy dominated by commercial interests. Witness his contemptuous remark about England's being a land of shopkeepers. Industry he was willing to encourage, especially when it made use of domestic raw materials. He offered a million francs for the invention of machinery that would enable France to use linen instead of cotton. In 1811, he went so far as to forbid the wearing of cotton in the royal palaces. Napoleon hated the idea that France should be dependent on foreign goods. In his belief that agriculture was the real source of a country's strength, he was a physiocrat. The sons of the peasantry made good soldiers, and a state primarily agrarian need fear no loss of outside sources of supply. But one must not forget that Napoleon had read Adam Smith. The Corsican's physiocracy was blended with a sort of laissez-faire industrialism.[6]

It seems beyond question that both the New Order and the Grand Design aim, though somewhat vaguely in the latter case, at world empire. In one instance, France is to be the favored country, the focal point for universal domination; in the other, it is to be Germany. The rest of the world is to consist of vassal states. The first step in both cases is to achieve political unity for Europe. This is to done by military conquest and by propaganda—the sword and the pen, the bayonet plus the printing press, the cannon's roar reënforced by the voice of the demagogue.

The Napoleonic administrative system, with its hierarchy of prefects, is essentially the same as the Nazi system of Reich Protectors and *Gauleiters*. Both systems are bureaucratic in principle and practice, are anti-parliamentarian by nature. The ultimate of centralization is the goal in each instance. The entire setup rests on the army as the final source of authority. Napoleon sought to apply his administrative system to all the vassal kingdoms, but found it difficult to hold them in line. The dynamism of the French Revolution so strengthened the subject peoples that they finally overthrew the Napoleonic empire. The Nazis are aware of a similar danger. As Hitler puts it: "Naziism is not an article for export." Other strong totalitarian states would endanger the plan of German empire. That is why weak governments in the hands of inefficient natives are encouraged in the subject lands, and why the fascist parties there are not allowed to become very strong.

Napoleon sought to reach beyond the status of dictatorship and legitimize his position. This explains his attempt to set up a dynasty, his marriage with a member of the Habsburg family. He surrounded France with a ring of vassal states, governed by kings who secured their crowns through his power. These states were to possess no real sovereignty.

The Napoleonic claim to the creation of a federation of European states was a fiction. His talk of federation was merely a device to conciliate those accustomed to autonomy.

Along with his administrative system Napoleon sought to impose the *Code*. In his opinion this legal system would consolidate the political unity of Europe. To him it was perfection, the embodiment of European civilization (and of bourgeois, familial, and propertied values). What was good for Frenchmen was good for all peoples. As he expressed it: "There is after all little difference between one nation and another."

The *Code Napoléon* illustrates a significant difference between the New Order and the Grand Design. The *Code* is a synthesis of the Old Regime and the French Revolution. It combines liberty and order, civil rights and governmental prescription. There is nothing remotely like it in the Nazi System. Force* rather than law is the guiding principle of the Third Reich. Justice is whatever is decreed by the hierarchy of *Führers*.

An analysis of the political aspects of the Grand Design must take account of Napoleon's education. It is well to remember that he was a student of the *philosophes*. From these eighteenth-century thinkers derives his contempt for democracy. He believed in enlightened despotism because it met the need for authority as well as the need for reform. It is evident that his ultimate goal was the complete elimination of the elective principle.† He agreed with Voltaire in the latter's statement that he would "rather be ruled by one lion than by a hundred rats."

The New Order is the complete negation of individualism. The Nazis regard the French Revolution as the beginning of modern degeneration. Democracy is a decadent political system, utterly out of place in the twentieth century.

* Force as used here involves all the means by which man is able to terrorize his fellows.

† See the model constitutions he drew up for the kingdoms of Westphalia and Naples.

What is required today is an authoritarian regime capable of maintaining order in a world given to conflict. Those capable of triumphing in this struggle are destined to rule.

Let there be no question that Napoleon was as contemptuous of the masses as Hitler. Witness his reprimand of his brother Jerome: "If you listen to public opinion you will achieve nothing. If the people refuse their own good fortune [i.e., the dictates of Napoleon] they are anarchists, criminals, and their punishment is the first duty of the ruler."[7] In the case of both Napoleon and Hitler there is a sort of "benevolent" authoritarianism from above, coupled with a real contempt and fear of the masses. But in the one instance there is a self-conscious, "bourgeois" authoritarian, and in the other a vague, "socialist," hyper-racialist fanatic.

Despite theoretical claims to a New Order, the Hitler regime is in some ways much like the Napoleonic empire. One notes the recurrence of the same old political form: dictatorship seeking some form of "divine right" justification. Napoleon sought to have the world consider him the successor of Charlemagne and the Caesars. The Nazi regime finds its "divine" justification in its racial creed. Herein it differs fundamentally from the Napoleonic system. The Nazis believe the Germans are the Master-Race, destined to rule the world. All other peoples are slated for varying degrees of slavery. The French of the Napoleonic era regarded themselves as a superior nationality, but did not possess the fierce intolerance of other races which characterizes the Nazis. Although the Corsican conqueror did not like the Jews, there was no "scientific" anti-Semitism in the Napoleonic system. Indeed, Napoleon's conquest of Germany liberated the Jew from the ghetto and raised him to the status of citizen.

Racialism is a more accurate description of the Nazi goal than nationalism. Even the all-powerful state is but a means to the supreme end—the attainment of world power by the Master-Race. Only members of this Master-Race are entitled to the benefits of world domination. There is no recognition of the common humanity of peoples. The non-Teutonic nations are not to be "Germanized." These "lesser breeds" are to be either exterminated or enslaved.

Within the Master-Race itself there is to be a hierarchy. Those who rule constitute the Master-Class; the other members of the race occupy the subordinate positions. This Master-Class is not a caste; one does not attain such status by inheritance. It is, in theory, a natural aristocracy, based upon ability to rule. One is reminded of Napoleon's "career open to talent," of his famous statement that "every private carries a marshal's baton in his knapsack."

The Nazi racial policy leads inevitably to difficulties with the church. Neither of the dictators was able to reconcile Christianity and totalitarianism. The difference was fundamental, for Christianity regards the individual as immortal and the state as not. Under Bonapartism and Nazism the reverse is true. This is a fact of cardinal political importance. It explains the affinity of democracy and Christianity for each other. Both Napoleon and Hitler insisted that their subjects put loyalty to their regimes above loyalty to a church or to God. Both were incapable of comprehending Kant's dictum: "The true moral principle is to treat humanity as an end and never only as a means." Both dictators made treaties with the Pope to gain the support of the Catholic Church, but both broke their agreements when the church barred the road to absolute power. Both were regarded as the arch-enemies of religion and denounced as Antichrist in person. Yet both found priests to praise them as the saviors of civilization.

Napoleon was reared in the Catholic faith and died in it, but his career was that of a practical atheist. He was willing to allow his subjects to profess whatever faith they chose; each sect could find its own route to Heaven. He believed that religion was necessary in order to keep the masses in order, but he had no intention of allowing it to interfere with his empire. As he expressed it: "How can you have order in a State without religion? Society cannot exist without inequality of wealth, and inequality of wealth cannot exist without religion. . . . Religion is the vaccine of the imagination; it preserves the latter from all dangerous and absurd beliefs. . . . If you take the faith away from the people you have only highway robbers."[8] The churches were to concern themselves with serving the state. In fact, he sought to achieve what had always tended to happen under the Bourbons—to make the church serve as a department of the state. Hitler also was reared as a Catholic, but his conception of the rôle of the church is quite different from that of Napoleon. Real loyalty is to the racial creed, which demands that the Nordic suffer no sense of sin. He is to be a realist, unrestrained by concepts of mercy, pity, humanitarianism. In such a system Christ is a pernicious influence. In place of Christianity there is a religion of Blood and Race. This new faith finds its Bible in *Mein Kampf*, its prophet in Hitler.

There are significant differences between Napoleon's social policy and that of the Nazis. Napoleon sought to attach the property-owning classes to his regime by guaranteeing their possessions and their profits. The social hierarchy he set up was based primarily upon wealth. As the years went by, he turned more and more toward the idea of landed aristocracy. His agrarian prejudices led him to believe that only with such support could his system endure. The increasing use of the old nobility in the governmental service he explained with the statement: "Only these know how to serve." What he was seeking was the legitimization of his position so that he might found a dynasty. The aristocracy was not to be independent of the dictator, for Napoleon had no intention of returning to feudalism. His conception of aristocracy was essentially one of talent, to which went quite naturally the rewards of wealth and position. "Aristocracy always exists," he said, "destroy it in the nobility, it removes itself immediately to the rich and powerful houses of the middle class."[9]

Napoleon's social policy in the vassal states was to recruit support for his system among the bourgeoisie and the peasants. This is clearly stated in a letter to his brother Jerome, who was ruler of Napoleon's model state in Germany, the Kingdom of Westphalia: "To speak quite plainly, I count more on the efforts of these persons [bourgeoisie and peasants] for extending and solidifying this monarchy than on the greatest victories."[10] To win over these classes he extended the benefits of the French Revolution: civil equality, religious liberty, abolition of tithes and feudal dues, confiscation and sale of church property, suppression of the guilds, a great increase in the number of government jobs, an honest and efficient administration. This social policy was incarnate in the *Code Napoléon;* that is why he was so keen on introducing the *Code* throughout Europe.

There are some who regard Napoleon as a great liberator in the sphere of social policy. It is true that he did not attempt to undo the Revolution's destruction of feudalism; and that, to serve his own ends, he extended this destruction to much of the rest of Europe. But it must be remembered that he restored slavery in the French colonies, that he refused to proclaim the end of serfdom in Russia, that he established a new nobility (in large part hereditary), and that he reëstablished primogeniture for the estates of this new aristocracy. For the professions, he favored monopolistic "orders," which resembled in many ways the guilds of the Old Regime. Let us be sure to add that the wealthy were allowed to purchase exemption from military service. A man so egotistical as Napoleon never could have become a liberator in any enduring sense. It was as Goethe said: "Napoleon, who lived wholly in the ideal, could not consciously grasp it."

The underprivileged of Europe were encouraged to welcome Napoleon, the conqueror who promised to destroy feudalism and bring the blessings of the French Revolution. In similar fashion Hitler proclaims that his mission is to free the masses from the evils of capitalism and plutocracy. Both dictators reënforced their power politics with the explosive force of social revolution. In each case they were careful to choose for their programs the solution of the most pressing problems of the age. Napoleon held out the promise of ending class distinctions based upon heredity; Hitler extends a claim to end the menace of unemployment.

Napoleon came from the petty nobility of Corsica, but his status in France as a youth was bourgeois. This probably explains his antagonism toward feudalism. He rose to power through bourgeois aid, but he was not really bourgeois at heart. He desired position as well as authority. Never could he have maintained himself in power had he not guaranteed the privileges obtained by the property owners through the French Revolution. That is why he was careful to preserve a regime which was capitalistic in orientation. An opportunist, seeking every avenue which would increase his power, Napoleon attempted to appeal to all classes. Witness his concordat with the Pope to win over the Catholics, his guarantee of land titles to win over those who had purchased confiscated property, his Legion of Honor to titillate the bourgeois élite, his efforts to assure hegemony in Europe to the business interests of France, his subsidies to members of the old aristocracy. His statements of policy were deliberately confusing in order to win both radical and conservative support. He promised to protect capital against both radical Jacobinism and aristocratic tyranny; to the masses, he posed as a liberator.

Hitler came from the petty bourgeoisie, but was forced to live as a proletarian. His experience made him hate the class struggle, made him an enemy of Marxism. Hence the Nazi party drew its strength in the beginning from the petty bourgeoisie, and Hitler was ushered into power with the aid of the upper bourgeoisie. Nonetheless, his goal is the destruction of the old class structure and the substitution of a new system based upon race and service to the Party. Income and social prestige are to be determined by the value of this service. The new Master-Class will hold the status of landed aristocrats. The remaining members of the Party (which will embrace every worthy German) will constitute a new middle class. Underneath will be the hewers of wood and the drawers of water, those barred forever from participation in the government, the slaves. Systematic depopulation will remove such of the subject aliens as are unnecessary.

It is interesting to speculate on the eternal historical question of whether personality or circumstance determines the course of events. Probably the question of "either-or" is misleading; in all likelihood, what happens is the result of interaction between men and the mass movements which lie behind them. It has been pointed out that behind Alexander the Great lay the expansive force of Greek culture, behind Charlemagne the power of Christianity. Napoleon undoubtedly represents the dynamism of the French Revolution. He capitalized upon French nationalism and upon France's belief that it had a new dispensation to give the world, a new way of life based upon "liberty, equality, and fraternity."

We must face the question of what dynamic force lies behind Hitler. Nationalism is certainly a part of the story. Still another factor is an intolerant racial pride, with its concomitant racial hatred. Involved, too, is a demand for social justice, a revolution of the many against exploitation by the few. This is not to say that Hitler is an apostle of the square deal—far from it. But there is behind the Nazi movement this blind inchoate demand of the masses for a better life. It lies behind other revolutions; the Russian of 1917, the Chinese of 1911, the Italian of 1922, the American New Deal. Let us note here that this insistent pressure of the masses does not guarantee that the revolutions it produces always achieve the desired goal. Revolutions have been betrayed; in fact they usually are, for it is their nature to be betrayed. The gulf between the real and the ideal is vast. Yet this popular pressure continues despite setbacks. Those who seek power, whether by autocratic or by democratic methods, ignore it at their peril. Ultimately, it will achieve its goal; and governments will then serve the purposes of their peoples. The plans of their would-be masters, Latin, Teutonic, or what-not, will prove of no avail.

It is by contrasting Napoleon with Hitler that one realizes how menacing the latter really is. Napoleon operated within a frame of reference which liberals regard as good, or at least potentially good. Hitler, on the other hand, is truly the "voice of destruction" for democratic liberalism. Those who adhere to the principles of the French Revolution are skeptical of the "good" which Hitler claims to represent, and are certain that he stands for much that is indisputably evil. This is the essential conclusion which one draws from a comparison of the New Order and the Grand Design.

# Impressment during the American Revolution

*ELIZABETH COMETTI*
*Instructor in History*

*Our fears of despotism seem to be carried too far for a time of War and may in the end deprive us of that Liberty we are contending for & bring on us the most abject slavery. The histories of all nations teach* [*us*], *that no people can enjoy happiness long that will not part with a small portion of their Liberty for the benefit of the Society in which they live.*[1]

WHEN Governor Benjamin Harrison of Virginia wrote these words he might well have been referring not merely to impressment during the American Revolution, but to emergency legislation in general. Extraordinary times have always called for extraordinary measures, and for this reason impressment was not a new or an unexpected practice in 1782. Under the name of great purveyance this prerogative had been exercised in feudal times in respect to provisions, transport, and, to a limited extent, labor. Later, when the name was changed to something more euphonious to English ears, the characteristics remained the same: impressment still constituted a purchase of goods or services under compulsory powers.

During the American Revolution both belligerents resorted to impressment of goods and men in varying degrees. The British never hesitated to plunder the countryside or to institute "hot presses" of sailors in those towns where their fleet was anchored, but the embattled states could not generally afford to be too opportunistic in regard to the latter practice, lest they be accused of those same acts of tyranny laid at the door of their former sovereign. Nevertheless, on two occasions Rhode Island did authorize the impressment of ". . . Seamen, transient foreign Persons, and [those] not Inhabitants of this or any of the United States, and not inlisted into the Service of this State, or the Continent. . . ."

But almost immediately these acts were repealed and pains were taken to justify them on grounds of necessity.[2] In the autumn of 1780, when Virginia's coast was harassed by enemy vessels, the executive of that state was empowered to issue warrants for the impressment of seamen. Unlike Rhode Island, the crews of foreign vessels or those belonging to sister states were not to be disturbed, and the period of service was limited to nine months.[3] Had the American navy been larger, it is possible that impressment of seamen might have been the rule instead of the exception; but conditions being what they were, this was not the case.

For land operations men were sometimes impressed into the transportation service, which was ineffably clumsy and hopelessly disorganized. In the southern states Negroes were used for fatigue duty, especially in those regions where roads were impassable to teams. Slaves were also employed as "artificers" and for constructing batteries. When the assigned work entailed considerable risks, as in the latter instance, each slave was carefully evaluated in order that the owner might not suffer loss without due compensation. Despite this regard for the sacred right of property, the owners were not beyond using dilatory tactics to avoid furnishing their quotas of slaves.[4]

The crying need of the army, however, was not men but property in the form of supplies and means of transporting them. Consequently the bulk of the impressment laws passed by Congress and the various states dealt almost exclusively with the taking of goods. Compared with the states, the powers of Congress in this respect were exceedingly limited, indeed scarcely more than of a recommendatory nature. For example, in November, 1775, Congress, itself unable to act in the emergency, urged the New England legislatures to authorize General Washington to take by force any needed means of transportation.[5] As the war progressed, impressment became more and more frequent, and in order to check the numerous abuses which were producing friction between the civil and military authorities, it became necessary to maintain a semblance of uniformity regarding the method of exercising the prerogative.

A step in this direction was taken by Congress on February 22, 1777, when it recommended to the several legislatures a mode of impressing the means of transportation. Since subsequent state regulations conformed, for the most part, to this pattern suggested by Congress, the report merits some attention. By it, justices of peace, receiving an order from the commander-in-chief, from any general, from any field or commissioned officer, from a quartermaster-general, or from deputies in his department, were required to issue warrants to the various constables near the line of march. Such constables were obligated to round up the available means of transportation and drivers for the use of the army. In the event that the justices, constables, or owners refused to acquiesce, they were liable to mild fines. More important, in the light of what actually happened, was the provision that the commander-in-chief might grant a press warrant in case the justices refused to coöperate. The report also included regulations regarding the number of transports which might be impressed for each regiment and the price allowed the inhabitants for their use. Finally, the action of Congress was to have the force of law until the states themselves should legislate on the subject.[6]

The inevitable abuses engendered by coercion, coupled with jealousy for their rights, induced the states to modify the above method of procedure by more stringent regulation. As necessity broadened the scope of impressment to include forage, food, clothing, pasturage, billets, building materials of all kinds, firewood, and a miscellany of other indispensables, irregularities quite naturally increased commensurately. The following measures indicate how some of the states sought to check the power of the military. Except in cases of sudden necessity, Delaware forbade the impressment of water transport without authorization by the state executive or the commander-in-chief of the state.[7] Pennsylvania, long the seat of war, established an elaborate system for requisitioning the transportation resources of the state. Instead of direct impressment, the military was obliged to apply to a state wagon-master-general who, in turn, would order his regional assistants to summon waggoners in rotation. If the latter refused to obey the order, the civil and not the military authority applied to a justice for warrants.[8] Through the vigilance of the Pennsylvania executive and public, this act certainly accomplished its avowed purpose of restraining the military. When General Sullivan rashly mentioned impressment in an application for means of transportation, he was bluntly informed that despite inconveniences he would have to abide by the law. To be sure, this would involve delay; but the army had only itself to blame for having to suffer the consequences of past abuses.[9] Even members of Congress were censured for having the temerity to pass a resolution which disregarded the law. The solons, although they insisted that the crisis had warranted a "Vigorous Remedy," ate humble pie and admitted that the Pennsylvania law had been violated.[10]

As with most impressment laws, the above contained provisions for the suspension of the regular method of procedure in the event of a sudden emergency. Unfortunately, however, the condition warranting suspension was generally left undefined, an omission which gave rise to numerous irregularities. Indeed, Pennsylvania found the provision so "inconvenient and prejudicial to the good people" of the state that no person, not even the commander-in-chief "under any pretence whatsoever" could impress except by warrant from the executive council signed by the President or Vice-president.[11]

Rhode Island went even further. Her legislature not only adopted restrictive measures, but also defined a state of emergency, with peculiar results, as will be seen. The act provided that when a quartermaster was unable to buy supplies and transport from the inhabitants, he should apply to the state executive or justices for a warrant, directed to the sheriff, ordering any person who was thought to have the needed goods to appear at court. If, on examination, it was found that the person possessed the specified articles and he could "without very great inconvenience spare the same," the quartermaster might proceed with impressment. The military, however, could use "all their Force and Power . . . when and at any Time the Enemy should actually land upon the Main, and . . . make Incursions into the Country."[12] According to the interpretation of doughty General Sullivan, this act was both ridiculous and dangerous. Only in one case could the interminable red tape prescribed by the law be dispensed with, i.e., when the enemy had actually landed and was proceeding into the country. "But," the disgusted General pointed out, ". . . this cannot take place, until they are completely and safely landed on the main; not even if their whole army was seen in boats rowing up with the river, should they give the most convincing proofs that their designs were against Providence, citations and hearings must go on, till they have actually landed in the town. . . ."[13] No doubt Sullivan felt happier when the act was repealed the following month.[14]

During and after the Yorktown campaign, Virginia saw fit to prohibit all impressments except by warrant from the executive, in case of actual invasion, or by sheriffs bringing criminals to the General Court. In this way she hoped to prevent Continental staff and military officers from commiting "great violences upon the property of the citizens on a pretense of a right to impress."[15] Unfortunately for the army, Virginians interpreted the act literally, and resisted all impressment without executive warrant, regardless of the circumstances. When application for a warrant was made to Governor Harrison, he was not always willing to acquiesce, because he believed that the state had already "been more oppressed in this way than any Country on earth."[16] In the fall and winter of 1781-1782 southern governors were inclined to place as strict construction upon impressment laws as possible. When Governor Rutledge of South Carolina curtly informed General Marion, "I know of no authority that any Continental officer, or any other person . . . has to impress in this state without a power from me . . . ,"[17] he was only expressing a mood common to most executives in the South.

But despite restrictive acts and gubernatorial vigilance, officialdom as a whole tried to coöperate with the army, at least as much as its constituents permitted. In 1779, for example, New York facilitated impressment by increasing the fines against recalcitrant inhabitants and by raising, at the same time, the pay of constables. The following year the fines were still further increased.[18] Both New York and New Jersey bluntly warned people who deliberately put their transport out of repair that such acts of sabotage would avail them nothing; they would have to pay for repairs as well as court costs.[19] New York's Governor Clinton went so far as to counsel artifice in order to assist the army in getting supplies. "I am sensible," he wrote, "of the Difficulties . . . but by employing secret Agents to treat with such as you suspect have Cattle for sale under an idea of dealing in specie you may promote the Business [impressment] & on this Occasion it will be justifiable."[20] Toward the end of the war, when most emergency legislation had either lapsed or been repealed, several states enacted laws to prevent suits from being instituted against men charged with having committed irregularities in the course of executing impressment orders.[21]

Although some individuals probably deserved judicial protection, others were doubtless guilty of flagrant and avoidable abuses. With a hungry and not too well-disciplined soldiery it was easy enough for foraging parties to degenerate into plundering expeditions. Even General Greene, whose experiences in the quartermaster department convinced him of the necessity for impressment, was forced to admit that the American soldiers committed acts of plunder and violence comparable to those of the Hessians.[22] When an outraged Pennsylvanian stated somewhat quaintly, "I conceive it to be my Duty to acquaint you that I conceive I am no more master of anything I possess . . . ,"[23] he expressed the feeling of many who had sustained heavy damages to their property and had been forced to sell supplies at the point of a bayonet.

On the other hand, the so-called victims did not have an absolutely clear record. As a result of fluctuating prices, goods about to be impressed were sometimes evaluated by two or three disinterested inhabitants or justices of the peace. As might have been expected, these worthies, neighbors of the owners, were not averse to appraising the articles all too generously. Aware of this, Virginia, in November, 1781, prohibited the settlement of any claims not having been passed by the court and certified to the General Assembly, in order "to enable her to render justice to individuals and save the public from unjust demands and impositions." The following year final adjustment was placed in the hands of the auditors for public accounts and a number of commodities, ranging all the way from pickled beef to common laborers, received legislative evaluation.[24]

The frailties of human nature, however, were only mildly responsible for the evils of impressment. The root of the trouble was the increasingly deranged state of finances. As has been pointed out, although impressment implies compulsion, it does not exclude compensation. But compensation in sound currency is one thing and compensation in certificates of uncertain value is another. The woeful story of Revolutionary finance is too well known to require elaboration here. It is enough to say that impressment only served to increase the number of commissary and quartermaster certificates already in circulation and thus helped to create a tremendous debt. And when it is remembered that between the receipt of a certificate and the time of its payment the currency was depreciating with great rapidity, it is not difficult to understand why certificates were offered for sale at discount and magistrates often refused to execute impressment warrants unless the military officials were able to pay on the spot, which was rarely possible.[25]

In an effort to ease the people's burden, some states hit upon the dangerous expedient of making the certificates receivable for taxes. This only resulted in drying up the leading source of future revenue. Had the politicians possessed sufficient courage to tap new sources of revenue the situation might not have been so bad. But they feared the consequences of sweeping financial reforms.[26] In the spring of 1781, Quartermaster General Pickering wrote Congress that many inhabitants of New York had enough state certificates to pay for several years' taxes. Yet these people were obliged to continue selling goods in return for more certificates, this time certificates not receivable in taxes. Conditions were no better in the South. Virginians would not sell except on cash terms, and since the staff departments had no money, the only alternative was impressment. "I never saw a country so loaded with certificates as the State of Virginia," Pickering reported. "There is not an article scarcely that can be mentioned but what has been taken and nothing but a bare certificate left in payment even to breakfasts & dinners for officers, and likewise for many Soldiers. It is useless for the people to object to any such thing, because the soldiery have arms in their hands, & give necessity as a reason for impressing what they think proper."[27] When Virginia finally forbade all impressments, Governor Harrison jubilantly informed Congress that "the oppressive & tyrannical measure of impressment" would no longer be used and that the Continental army could look to Congress for supplies.[28] It should be pointed out, however, that Harrison wrote this after the crisis of the war had been passed.

It was indeed unfortunate that impressment should have borne so heavily on some states, while those far removed from the theatre of war suffered none of its disadvantages.

In the former group the civil authorities sought to appease the sincere patriots by discriminating against political and economic suspects—Tories, hoarders, forestallers. Washington not only approved but himself encouraged such a policy, especially in Pennsylvania, where the combined Quaker and Tory elements constituted a formidable bloc. But the characteristics of Toryism were not sufficiently distinct to preclude abuses on the part of those charged with impressment. Washington complained that "they go about the country, plundering whomsoever they are pleased to denominate Tories, and converting what they get to their own private profit and emolument."[29]

In the last analysis, the attitude of high military officials toward impressment was of supreme importance, for while exercising this prerogative, they had it in their power to flout the ideals of the Revolution and thereby to weaken the cause of independence. Fortunately some of the army leaders had had experience in civil affairs and were the first to realize that the average man will lose enthusiasm for the end if he suspects the means. More fortunate was the fact that no one was more tender of the feelings of the inhabitants than the most influential man in the army, George Washington. Scores of impressment orders issued from his headquarters indicate this beyond a doubt: if coercion must be employed, they read, spread out the burden; prevent waste and abuse; execute orders in the least grievous manner giving the inhabitants certificates for everything taken; unauthorized impressment will not be tolerated; discriminate between the well affected and disaffected, taking from the former with a more sparing and indulgent hand; use delicacy and discretion. Plainly, these are not the injunctions of a militarist. In 1780, when the states lagged in furnishing their respective requisitions for the maintenance of the army, Washington urged them to comply lest the American cause should be ruined by an army of plunderers instead of protectors.[30] To the soldiers he said: "It is Irksome to mention and even painful . . . to Reflect how disgraceful and derogatory it would be to the reputation of an Army who are the Assertors of Freedom as well as of the Rights of Humanity and of individuals should they ever be guilty of plundering the minutest article."[31]

In emergencies, however, Washington did not hesitate to order impressment even when he had no authority to do so. But before deviating from the law, he would generally try persuasion, gentle at first, arbitrary only as a last resort.[32] During the terrible winter of 1779-1780 some of the New Jersey magistrates refused to execute impressments. In January Washington ordered his officers to approach the reluctant justices with a personal message describing the wants of the army. Then he added: "You will at the same time delicately let them know, that you are instructed, in case they do not take up the business immediately, to begin to impress the Articles called for, throughout the County."[33] Either from motives of patriotism or fear, the justices and inhabitants responded to the plea of Washington and sold generously. These same tactics were successfully used again when justices once more refused to coöperate. As Washington posed the alternatives, impressment or dissolution of the army, they could hardly do otherwise.[34]

Despite Washington's efforts to be moderate or firm, as the occasion demanded, he was sometimes upbraided for the one or the other. In December, 1777, when the inept Congress invested Washington with dictatorial powers, that body expected him to make the most of them. Far from being rendered happy by this show of confidence, the Commander-in-Chief wrote:

> I confess, I have felt myself greatly embarrassed with respect to a vigorous exercise of Military power. An Ill placed humanity perhaps and a reluctance to give distress may have restrained me too far. But these were not all. I have been well aware of the prevalent jealousy of military power, and that this has been considered as an Evil much to be apprehended even by the best and most sensible among us.[35]

The governors, on the other hand, were forever complaining to him about military coercion.[36] Governor Reed of Pennsylvania penned veritable sermons on the subject.[37] Harrassed by two fires of criticism, and meriting neither, Washington mournfully wished that his troops might, like chameleons, live on air, or like bears, suck their paws for sustenance.[38]

The responsibility for the lack of system did not devolve on Washington. A weak Congress held the ties which bound together thirteen jealous states. As the difficulties increased Congress relinquished what powers it had, with the result that "all the business [was] now *attempted* . . . by a timid kind of recommendation from Congress to the States."[39] In vain did Washington passionately assert that there must not be thirteen councils, that Congress should have absolute authority in matters of war. The surrender of powers continued, but the lesson was not lost on such men as the young James Madison and Alexander Hamilton. Nor did Washington forget it. Before another decade had passed, mutual suffering and a common victory followed by mutual problems and responsibilities were to weld the states into one young and vigorous whole. In future crises there would still be emergency legislation. But there would also be one source of authority to coördinate the sincere efforts of the people and to hasten the day of peace.

# The Colonial Status of the South

*BENJAMIN BURKS KENDRICK*

*Chairman of the Department of History and Political Science*

IF IT IS TRUE that the South is "the Nation's No. 1 economic problem," the fundamental historical explanation of that condition is to be found in the fact that for more than three centuries this region, in greater or less degree, has occupied the status of a colony. Generally colonials produce raw materials which they exchange on unfavorable terms with citizens of the imperial power for manufactured goods. As a result they fall increasingly into debt to those with whom they trade. Meanwhile, the outside creditors often invest some, or all, of their balances in the colonial area. These investments in the old days were mostly in agricultural real estate, enterprises for trapping and fur trading, and companies for the exploitation of timber and mineral wealth. Outsiders also generally owned the means of transportation and collected the freight on incoming and outgoing traffic. In the past seventy-five years, outside investments, while continuing in some of the older forms, have gone into internal transportation and communication companies, urban real estate and mortgages thereon, financial organizations and—perhaps of greatest importance today—into manufacturing. To this general pattern the South has almost perfectly conformed. At the present time the productive property of this region is largely owned by persons living outside its bounds. The fact that the owners are citizens of the same sovereign nation as are the people of the South, has, in some manner, obscured the fact of the region's colonial status.

The purposes underlying this interpretative essay are: first, to suggest that the colonial status of the South might have been ended permanently by the American Revolution if, after that event, it had become an independent sovereignty instead of uniting with the Northeast in the United States of America under the Constitution of 1787; second, that having failed to take advantage of the opportunity offered by the so-called "Critical Period," it thereafter became too late to remedy the situation either by internal compromises or by secession; and third, to show that finance capitalism and imperialism continuously tightened their grip upon the region from the close of the Civil War until the advent of the great depression of the 1930's.

Even as early as 1600, the rising middle classes in Great Britain were aware that it was a good deal more profitable to engage in manufacturing, shipping, and buying and selling than it was in producing raw materials. This awareness explains why persons of the middle class should have concerned themselves with the establishment of an American colonial empire. In the colonies the "superfluous" populations of England and other western European countries could be put to work producing raw materials which were sold at a low price to merchants, transported for a good profit by shipowners, fabricated with considerable gain to manufacturers, and resold at home, abroad, and to the colonists at a dear price, again by the merchants. It would be unfair to imagine for a moment that the gentlemen adventurers who established the London Company to carry into practical effect these ideas were in any sense parasitical. As a matter of fact, without their initiative, enterprise, and willingness to take a gambler's chance, the colonization of America would have been long delayed. History records that these first adventurers actually lost most of the money they advanced. But in the long run English merchants as a class did gain not only from the Virginia colony but also from the four other plantations which by 1733 dotted the Atlantic coast from the Chesapeake Bay to the St. Mary's River.

Between 1607 and 1776, there elapsed 169 years—a period slightly longer than that since 1776. During these five or six generations, there evolved in the South some colonists who became owners of broad acres and many slaves. But these southern landowners who grew tobacco or rice for Old World markets, and in addition shipped abroad timber, naval stores, and a variety of other raw materials, were always aware that they were netting but little beyond a fair living from their investments and their entrepreneurial efforts. Year by year their debts increased until on the eve of the Revolution Thomas Jefferson could say truthfully of himself and his neighbors that they were merely "a species of property, annexed to certain mercantile houses in London." And later Oliver Wolcott could say: "It is a firmly established opinion of men well versed in the history of our revolution, that the Whiggism of Virginia was chiefly owing to the debts of the planters." Over a century later, the historical researches of Arthur Meier Schlesinger and other scholars largely corroborated the truth of Jefferson's and Wolcott's statements.

One of the first sovereign acts of the new states was the confiscation of debts to British merchants and the expropriation of the property of British subjects, including that of native Tories. This exercise of the power to confiscate, be it noted, was one method employed by the colonial planters and merchants to escape from their colonialism. In New England and the Middle States the escape was permanent. Moreover, by gaining control of the commercial and financial policies of the new general government, the merchants, manufacturers, shipowners, and money-lenders of those states were eventually able to replace the similar groups in England in the exploitation of producers of raw materials and agricultural products not only in their own area but also in the South. Therefore, since the Southerners were destined for at least another century to continue as almost entirely agricultural producers and as purchasers of fabricated articles, it can be argued that it would have been better for the region to have relied principally upon Old England instead of upon New England as a source of supply of manufactured goods. For a century at least, Old England could have sold the South better goods for less money than New England was able to do. The terms of trade would have been unfavorable in either case, but it is more than probable that they would have been somewhat less so had the southern states remained economic dependencies of Great Britain.

From this it does not follow that the revolt of the South against England was not entirely justifiable on other grounds, for it was both reasonable and just for the members of the southern elite to desire for themselves honorable positions in social and political life. This understandable and natural ambition was an even more dynamic factor than debts in transforming such fundamental conservatives as the Habershams, the Pinckneys, the Johnsons, the Washingtons, and the Carrolls into revolutionists. Moreover, it was right, that, in consultation with their constituents, they should wish to formulate and direct their own domestic and foreign policies without regard to British Tory interests and opinions. Since a war was necessary for them to attain their objectives they were wise to ally themselves with their neighbors to the north and with France in order to assure the winning of that war.

But their northern neighbors and the French monarchy were actuated by a different set of motives from their own. With the latter, they entered into a military alliance which the French hoped and expected would eventuate in their becoming dependencies of France instead of England, when once the war was over. In this expectation the Gallic ally, as is well known, was disappointed. With the North, the South made a verbal compact, later formalized in the Articles of Confederation, which rendered mutual assistance possible without calling into question the sovereignty of the states. When commercial, financial, and speculative interests found this loose federation too weak to serve their purposes and began moving for a stronger central government, the Southerners should have been as wary of them as they had been of the British and French.

The foregoing statement brings up the delicate question of "historical relativity." "Historical relativity" places the historian dealing with the actions of men of a past epoch under obligation to do so not in the light of his own time but in that of the era with which he is concerning himself. Some thirty years ago, Charles A. Beard in his *An Economic Interpretation of the Constitution* and his subsequent *Economic Origins of Jeffersonian Democracy* proved to the satisfaction of most open-minded students that, in large measure, the Constitution was the handiwork of a revolutionary minority bent upon safeguarding and promoting the interests of commercial, manufacturing, and financial groups. Such groups were located almost entirely in the North, but they received the support and temporary alliance of southern plantation owners and speculators in western lands.

The keen political instinct of small farmers in general, and of the piedmont South in particular, warned them that the newly proposed Federal government would not be to their benefit. In North Carolina the small farmers were able to prevent ratification on the first test, while in Virginia they might have been successful in doing so had not some of their delegates, when subjected to pressure in the convention, apparently regarded their election promises as mere "campaign oratory." Even in South Carolina and Maryland their opposition was well known and articulate. In Georgia, where a temporarily exposed position made fear a predominant emotion, there seems to have been little opposition to the new and stronger union; but Georgia counted for but little at that time, and in the end would have followed the lead of her four more northerly neighbors had she received such a lead.

According to Beard, some of the plantation owners stood for alliance with other propertied groups because they were suspicious of the radical tendencies of their own Westerners.

In the light of their own time and the experiences they had had with the British merchants, it seems reasonable to assume that they should have feared the western radicals less and the northern businessmen more, since these latter were little different from similar groups in England and Scotland. Indeed, some few southern leaders did just that. For instance, George Mason and Patrick Henry in Virginia, and Willie Jones and William Lenoir in North Carolina opposed ratification. But the influence of men like Washington and Madison outweighed these latter.* The influence of such men must have been out of all proportion to their numbers, and while it is to their credit that they were able to take a large view of the situation, it was not in the long run advantageous to themselves, their class, or their section that they did so. Doubtless, some of them hoped and expected that the South would become relatively as much a commercial, industrial, and financial section as the North.†

Were there good grounds for such hope? Had they been able to concentrate on just two facts, it seems that they should have answered this question in the negative. The first of these facts was the slave system, which by that time was firmly fixed on the South, despite the opinion of some historians who believe that only the evolution of cotton culture on a grand scale made the continuation of the slave system inevitable. Actually the Southerners were habituated to the institution and would have been loath to part with it even had they been convinced that it was financially unprofitable.

* With regard to Madison it is only fair to point out that, as revealed in his masterpiece, "Federalist, Number 10," no other man of his time perceived so clearly the influence of economic interests upon political principles and actions. Apparently his own intellectual honesty led him to believe that the Constitution would always be interpreted *strictly* and that the United States government would remain *federal* in a sense opposite to *central* or *national*.

† It is interesting to speculate on the position Jefferson would have taken on the Constitution had he been in the country in 1787-1788. It seems that consistency and his keen distrust of the "economic royalists" of his time would have demanded that he oppose it, had he been present. That he could have opened Madison's eyes (as he did later) to the danger latent in the Constitution is also probable. Together Jefferson and Madison, in all likelihood, could have prevented southern ratification.

This attitude can be accounted for partly by the fact that the question was more social than economic at almost all times, as the late Ulrich B. Phillips perhaps overemphasized. Since a good part of southern capital had to go into the ownership of labor, it could hardly have been expected that there would be much left over for commercial, manufacturing, and financial enterprises.

The second fact is that, other things being equal, men follow the line of least resistance. Even in the 1780's everyone knew that the South had an almost limitless hinterland adaptable to the slave-plantation system, and that such capital as might be accumulated would necessarily go into the exploitation of this hinterland. The historical accident that the land claims of wealthy Virginians were mostly north of the Ohio, rather than south of it, may have been determining, but of that no one can be sure.

By way of summary it may be said that indeed the decade of the 1780's was a "Critical Period." But for the South it was "critical" in a sense exactly opposite to that in which the phrase was employed by John Fiske a century later. Fiske as a philosophical representative of and spokesman for industrial and commercial interests saw that what did in fact take place very well *might not* have done so, and such an eventuality would have been "bad" for the system for which he was an intellectual spokesman. To the South the period was "critical" because what did happen was "bad," while the establishment of a separate southern confederacy at that time would have been "good."*

* The terms "good" and "bad," "right" and "wrong," are employed throughout this paper in no moral sense. Whether such moral or ethical "goods" as the greater glory of God, democracy, human happiness as a whole, or even the "greatest good for the greatest number" were promoted or retarded by the Constitution no one can say with certainty. In general, historians, even including southern historians, have proceeded on the assumption that all these ethical "goods" were served by the Constitution. With this assumption it is not necessary to quarrel. Using the words as terms in social dynamics then, rather than in morality or ethics, it may be stated that the Constitution was "good" for the development of a system of capitalism in which control is concentrated in relatively few hands, and "bad" for a system of agricultural and other small tangible personal property interests in which control is widely dispersed.

Had the Constitution of 1787-1789 not been ratified by the southern states it is almost a certainty that the eight states to the north of Maryland, and perhaps Maryland too, eventually would have provided themselves with *a* constitution substantially identical with *the* Constitution we know. Indeed, that very Constitution might well have gone into effect, for by its own terms it provided that it would become operative when ratified by nine states. Had Virginia steadfastly refused to ratify, it can readily be assumed that in a relatively short time she would have been joined by the two Carolinas and Georgia in establishing a southern confederacy. We may be sure that such a confederacy would have been aggressively expansionist and would have obtained Florida, Louisiana, Texas, and California in an even shorter time than they were actually secured by the United States. Be it remembered that it was the South which furnished the driving force for making these acquisitions when the Northeast was holding back. The southern confederacy would have provided by advantageous trade treaties for the sale of its agricultural and other raw materials in whatever markets seemed most desirable. That cotton, tobacco, and rice would have gone to northern markets in payment for fabricated materials is certain, but such trade would have been on much more favorable terms than was actually the case. The bulk of southern commerce, however, would have been with Great Britain and the countries of northwest Europe, for the reason that for a long time, at least, these countries manufactured better and cheaper consumers' goods than did the North. Moreover, there would have been few if any tariff duties to pay on imports, with the result that the differential between prices paid and prices received would not have been nearly so great as it actually was. In short, a separate confederate government would have harmonized much better with the economic and social life of the region than did that of the United States. And, *pari passu*, it can with almost equal certainty be maintained that the government of the United States, with the South out of it, would have harmonized with greater precision with the life of the northern region. Finally, the relations between North and South would have been much more peaceful and mutually respectful had each been an independent sovereignty from the start. This can be said if for no other reason than that it is hard to conceive of such relations being *worse* than they actually were during the long years lying between the enunciation and adoption of Hamilton's financial policies in 1789-1791 and the withdrawal of Federal troops from Louisiana and South Carolina in 1877. In fact, it is reasonable to suppose that there would have been no greater ill feeling and squabbling between the two countries than actually existed between the United States and Canada. The Potomac-Ohio line formed a fairly natural boundary on this side of the Mississippi, while the western boundary probably could have been fixed as well by treaty as was that between Canada and the United States in 1846.*

If we think of the adoption of the Constitution as a marriage between the two sections, we may consider the Revolution as a period of friendship formed for the duration of a common danger, while to the Confederation period we may assign the status of a formal engagement. Just as it is usually much less tragic to break an engagement than to dissolve a marriage, so likewise it would have been better for the South never to have entered into a union with the North than later to have sought a dissolution. Perhaps the same excuse may be made for her action as is sometimes made for a young bride— namely, that she was not aware of the seriousness of the step she was taking. Certainly if she had married in haste, there was ample leisure for repentance. And repentance began immediately.

With this remark we turn now to consider the second purpose of this paper, which is an examination of the question: Was a compromise of the interests of the two sections

* In this connection it may be stated with some dogmatism that relations with Canada would not have been so pleasant had that dominion once been a part of the United States and afterwards established its independence.

possible under the Constitution, and if not, was subsequent separation feasible? That the South was yoked in an unequal union became apparent with the adoption of the Hamiltonian financial schemes, aimed as they were at enriching and strengthening the commercial, industrial, and, above all, the financial interests which were concentrated in the larger cities of New England and the Middle States. It is true that Hamilton rationalized that these measures would be beneficial to small property and agricultural interests as well, but just here began that disingenuous sophistry which to this day has characterized spokesmen for business interests and which more straightforward and forthright persons have found so difficult to parry.* Of almost equal importance in aggrandizing commercial and financial interests at the expense of agricultural interests in general and of the South in particular, was the pro-British foreign policy of the Federalists. Already the moneyed men of the northern cities were linking their destinies with those of similar groups in England, who, since the days of the Glorious Revolution, had largely controlled the financial and foreign policies of the motherland. With these policies the Federalists pursued one which recently we have called "parallel action." Name this reason or instinct, it was sound. Equally sound was the pro-French attitude of most Southerners, for the French Revolution had proclaimed undying hatred of monopoly of all sorts and everlasting devotion to "security, liberty, property, and resistance to oppression." And for "property" we may read "small, tangible, real and personal property"—that is, the sort to which the South was devoted. In other words, both sides seem to have recognized their friends and enemies when they saw them.

To the leadership of the Republicans now came Jefferson, seconded by Madison, Monroe, and lesser leaders. If we return for a moment to our engagement, marriage, and divorce figure, we may with propriety lay down the further

* Splendid examples of the two types of argument are Hamilton's memorandum in support of the constitutionality of the Bank of the United States and Jefferson's in opposition.

elaboration of it by saying that if there is to be a divorce at all, it is better for it to come soon—preferably before there are any children (in this case, new states) to complicate matters. Jefferson had the choice of two policies. Either he could undertake to rally agrarian and small-property classes in the North to unite with his southern constituents to capture the central government and undo the Federalist policies, or he could disregard any potential allies in the North and endeavor to commit the South to separation. Indeed, Jefferson could and perhaps did regard these procedures not merely as alternatives but as sequentials. That is to say, if the former should fail, he could fall back on the latter. There is no doubt that his personal preference was for the former, but that he was willing to resort to secession the Kentucky Resolutions of 1799 seem to attest. It is extremely doubtful, however, whether Jefferson would have led a southern secession movement had he and his party failed of victory in 1800. Hamilton's estimate of Jefferson—that he was a man bold in theory but timid in action—is probably correct. And this estimate of Jefferson is even more true of his closest associate and successor, Madison. The compromising character of the administrations of both men as well as that of the third member of the triumvirate, Monroe, is further proof that the Virginia hegemony was Girondin in character and not Jacobin, as some Federalist contemporaries professed to believe.

Not only did Jefferson and his successors fail to undo most of the special privileges that the Federalists had bestowed upon the business interests, but before Madison's second administration was over the protective tariff principle had been firmly established, and the Second Bank of the United States, much stronger and more monopolistic than the first, had been chartered. This weak leadership, after having made a great show of kicking special privilege out the parlor door, was responsible for allowing it to sneak back through the kitchen door. So far had this process gone that in 1824 the John Quincy Adams-Henry Clay coalition gained possession of the government in the name of National Republicanism! For this denouement, in addition to the timid character of the Virginia leadership, two other factors were responsible: (1) Most of the younger Federalists, despairing of rejuvenating their party after its unheroic conduct in the War of 1812, went over to the Republicans carrying with them their Federalist principles. (2) Many of Jefferson's northern lieutenants were beginning to embrace such principles in response to the improving economic and social status of themselves and some of their constituents. The two groups quickly fused and formed a veritable "fifth column" within the Republican body.* From his point of vantage they were able to "bore from within" as the modern Communist phrase has it, and to play the ancient Roman game of *divide et impera*. For this game the abolitionists furnished bats, balls, and gloves, while good diamonds were found in the Louisiana Purchase and later in the Mexican Cession.

So much has been said about the antislavery movement—its origins, motives, and progress—that it would be supererogation to attempt here any original contribution to the discussion. For the purposes of this paper, however, it is necessary to make two or three observations on the subject. The antislavery movement sprang from two sources. In the first place, it was a handy and, in most cases, a relatively inexpensive method for members of a conscientious nonslaveholding middle class to pay their debts to God. Long before 1800 Quakers and similar sects had begun so to employ it. It was none other than the very moral John Stuart Mill who first made the observation that morality is primarily a middle-class virtue. The poor, said Mill, *cannot* afford to be moral whereas the rich *can* afford *not* to be. Like every other

* That Jefferson himself was not unaware of what was going on is attested by a letter he wrote in 1822 to Albert Gallatin and another in 1824 to Martin Van Buren. In the former he said: "Do not believe a word of it [that the lion and the lamb are lying down together]. The same parties exist now as ever did." In the letter to Van Buren he wrote: "Tories are Tories still, by whatever name they be called."

aphorism of general significance this one has plenty of exceptions in its specific application. The general truth of Mill's statement, however, is reasonably apparent. Members of antislavery societies were drawn almost exclusively from groups who, economically, were small property owners and who, religiously, stemmed from seventeenth-century English Puritanism—itself a middle-class movement.

In the second place, slavery collided head-on with the eighteenth-century dogma, so eloquently incorporated into our Declaration of Independence in the ringing phrases: "that all men are created equal, that they are endowed by their Creator with certain unalienable Rights, that among these are Life, Liberty and the pursuit of Happiness." This egalitarianism was taken seriously everywhere by small property owners, but in the South it was applied in fact, even from the first, only to whites, and also in theory after the formulation and general acceptance of the proslavery argument. In the North on the other hand, where the social problem of the Negro was either nonexistent or not acute, egalitarianism had no need to draw the color line. Indeed, the devotees of the dogma in that section came eventually to assert that the genuine article could be distinguished from the spurious by subjecting it to what we may call the color test. So far did this conceit go that even the author of the immortal Declaration himself came to be suspected and, by the extremists, openly accused, of blackhearted hypocrisy. Even before his death it was already apparent to the more discerning, including perhaps Jefferson himself, that a wedge in the shape of the slavery controversy was being driven between his followers in the North and those in the South. The point here is that while financial and industrial capitalists and their political henchmen did not forge the wedge, when they saw it already entering the body of the Jeffersonians, they did not neglect to give it some mighty mauling. *Divide et impera.*

In cleaving the body of Jeffersonianism the financial and

industrial groups did not intend to rive the body of the Union. So much "aid short of war" had they given to the abolitionists, however, that by 1860 the latter were able to drive the wedge home and split asunder not only the body of Jeffersonianism but also that of the Union itself. And so had ended in failure the effort begun by Jefferson and continued by other apostles of small property to create and maintain on a national scale a party which could and would hold in check the overgrown pretensions and overweening ambitions of the party of special privilege. That is to say, it had proved impossible to prevent industry and finance from becoming the mistresses instead of remaining, as the Jeffersonians desired, the handmaidens of agriculture and commerce.

During few if any of the first seventy years of the Federal Republic were the terms of trade between the South and the industrial and financial centers of the North in favor of the former. The colonialization of the South was proceeding slowly but surely. During the first fifty of these years it was mainly in the older sections of the South that the pinch was felt acutely. During these years, indeed, it was the existence of a vast southern hinterland into which the more hard-pressed citizens of the older South could escape that prevented such near-crises as the Nullification and Wilmot Proviso controversies from becoming real crises. In the last twenty years of the period the pinch tended to become widespread throughout the region. It was during this time that southern leaders came to adopt two policies as sequentials: (1) further extension of the southern hinterland; and in case of the failure of this policy to fall back on (2) secession and an independent southern confederacy which they believed could prevent the bankruptcy which stared many of their constituents in the face. Add to this the obloquy and contumely in which Southerners were held by many of the "best" people of the North, and there remains no wonder that the stroke for southern independence was finally made.*

* It should be pointed out in this connection that the source of inspiration

It was the British historian and publicist Lord Acton who once undertook to compress the nature of the American Civil War into an aphorism. "Secession," ran the noble saw, "was an aristocratic rebellion against a democratic government." Except for the fact that a relatively few large plantation owners gave tone to and, in some degree, controlled social and political life in the South, and hence lent color to the aristocratic picture, the almost exact opposite of the Acton dictum is the truth. There is no need to labor this point, but it is pertinent to stress the fact that democracy, as a social and political system, arose with and flourished upon that sort of capitalism where private property was widely distributed, individually owned, and personally managed.* This was the character of the southern economic system previous to 1860. Even the so-called "poor whites" were seldom tenants. Manufactories, commercial enterprises, and financial institutions conformed to the pattern as well as did farms and plantations. Absentee ownership in any of these sorts of business was the exception rather than the rule. But as has been already emphasized, the South, even when its influence in Washington was considerable, was never able to control the terms of its domestic and foreign trade nor the money system in which trade was carried on. Consequently a new colonialism was taking place. But unity in the South, although greater in 1860 than ever before, was still far from

---

for the rising northern literati (especially those of New England) came to be the antislavery crusade. In addition to the preachers whose service of God was more and more equated with opposition to slavery, the theme song of the orators, poets, essayists, and novelists was subsequently expressed by Mrs. Howe in the lines:

> In the beauty of the lilies
> Christ was born across the sea,
> With a glory in his bosom that transfigures you and me;
> As he died to make men holy, let us die to make men free,
> While God is marching on.

Under such circumstances a "holy" war was inevitable. Sooner or later moderate men would be in a hopeless minority and be castigated as Copperheads—the "Appeasers" of that day. The comparison *is not* mine.

* Conversely, democracy as a way of social and political life may well be doomed when ownership and management is highly concentrated in the impersonal corporate form.

complete. This lack of unity was the most important single factor contributing to the ultimate defeat of the South.

> There is a tide in the affairs of men,
> Which, taken at the flood, leads on to fortune;
> Omitted, all the voyage of their life
> Is bound in shallows and in miseries.

The flood tide of 1787 was omitted: and the voyage which before the Civil War was "bound in shallows and in miseries," has since that event continued to be so bound.

For a decade or more after the Civil War the North undertook to rule the "conquered provinces" of the South by means of northern adventurers and southern "loyalists" whose political power rested upon universal Negro suffrage. Such rule needed to be buttressed constantly by Federal military force, for the "political potential" of carpetbaggers, scalawags, and Negroes was not equal to that of the former Confederates even in their pitifully weakened postwar condition. Such immature, brutally direct, and crassly inept imperialism, however camouflaged by such propaganda terms as "equality," "democracy," and "loyalty," sooner or later was bound to antagonize a sufficient number of nonimperialist elements in the North to spell its doom. And so it happened in 1877. The significance of the great compromise of that year turned out to be this: No longer would the northern imperialists undertake to rule the South by their own henchmen; on their part, the native southern elite would guarantee the protection of northern imperialist interests in the region.

This more mature policy worked exceedingly well. During the following half century, ownership of transportation, communication, financial, manufacturing, mining, and finally distributing corporations came to be largely held in the great cities of the Northeast, especially New York. Northern corporations and individuals owned most of the certificates of public indebtedness issued by the states, counties, and municipalities of the South. Likewise mortgages on southern agricultural and urban property were largely held in the

North. The profits on the insurance business done in the South were channeled off to New England and New York. While the total number of businessmen in the South was ever increasing, the proportion who were independent owners of small businesses was constantly decreasing. In short, southern businessmen were becoming mere agents and factors for northern principals. In the last quarter century the process has been accelerated. The World War, the era of "Coolidge Prosperity," the depression of the 1930's—each in its own way was a contributory factor. Today the subordination of all ordinary production to "defense" production, concentrated as it is in a few score great corporations, threatens the final ruin of such small businesses as still remain.

With the major part of income derived from profits, dividends, interest, and rent being siphoned out of the region to dwellers in the metropolises of the Northeast, the southern people were left to live mainly on wages, salaries, commissions, and other forms of income of similar nature. From studies made by Clarence Heer and others we know that these types of income were low in the South, relative to similar sorts of income outside this region. Necessarily this was so, not only because of the drain occasioned by payment of "invisible" items, but also because the South continued to be primarily a producer of raw materials and the coarser types of manufactured goods. This meant that the prices for which agricultural commodities were sold were much lower than prices paid for fabricated articles. In short, the southern people were obliged to work relatively more and more for less and less.

By the mid-1920's the second cycle of southern colonialism had made a full revolution. The articulate political people of the South were the businessmen. To them the press and professions were largely subservient. In maintaining their ascendancy they were greatly aided by all sorts of national associations of businessmen, such as chambers of commerce, so-called service clubs, and the like. The policies promulgated by such organizations emanated largely, if not entirely, from the great centers of finance capitalism and imperialism. The burden of their propaganda was that the interests of all businessmen were parallel to, if not identical with, those of the financiers. On a national scale the magazines, the movies, and finally the radio carried the propaganda of the vested interests into almost every nook and cranny of the land. In the Northeast and especially in the West there was considerable organized opposition to the avalanche, but in the South there was almost none. Hence we are confronted with a paradox more amazing and ironical than any ever conjured by the imagination of Gilbert and Sullivan. The people of the South, who all their lives had suffered deprivation, want, and humiliation from an outside finance imperialism, followed with hardly a murmur of protest leaders who, if indirectly, were nonetheless in effect agents and attorneys of the imperialists. Even our "Good Neighbors" and "Sister Democracies" to the south of us have never taken their medicine in so prone a position. Here from Virginia to Texas the Glasses and the Garners strove to "out-Mellon" Mellon. Never before in the history of this country had a single group so fully dominated public policy as did the finance capitalists during the "Golden Twenties." And nowhere was their dominance more complete than in their southern "colony."

That their direct rule was at least temporarily halted in the 1930's was not due to the activities of a well-organized opposition, but to the confusion into which the financiers were thrown by the utter failure of their own most cherished principles to work satisfactorily even for themselves. As a result, the election of 1932 brought into control of the Federal government a more strangely assorted group of men than Washington had seen since its establishment as the nation's capital. Under the spreading New Deal tent were gathered, from left to right, Communists, State Socialists, other varieties of Marxists, delegates from the camps of both radical and conservative labor, old-fashioned Democrats speaking for agriculture and small business, many kinds of reformers, representatives of the political "rings" of the great northern cities, and even a few "money-changers" whom Mr. Roosevelt had pledged himself to "scourge from the temple"—into the treasury, as it eventually turned out. To these multicolored groups the southern Democrats were added by the exigencies of party politics.

However, but few southern politicians were wholehearted supporters of New Deal reform measures, while many were either secretly or openly hostile to them. On the other hand, they voted almost unanimously in favor of the later Roosevelt foreign policies, as is clearly revealed by the vote in Congress on the crucial first Lend-Lease bill passed in the spring of 1941. For purposes of analysis, the country may be divided roughly into three sections: (1) The Northeast, consisting of the six New England states and the five Middle Atlantic states; (2) the South, consisting of the eleven ex-Confederate states, West Virginia, Kentucky, and Oklahoma; and (3) the West, consisting of the other twenty-three states. The vote on the bill by house and sections follows:

| *Section* | *For* | *Against* | *Absent or Not Voting* |
|---|---|---|---|
| SENATE | | | |
| Northeast | 16 | 6 | 0 |
| South | 25 | 1 | 2 |
| West | 20 | 25 | 1 |
| TOTALS | 61 | 32 | 3 |
| HOUSE | | | |
| Northeast | 81 | 46 | 2 |
| South | 119 | 5 | 1 |
| West | 61 | 119 | 1 |
| TOTALS | 261 | 170 | 4 |

Had the Southerners voted on the bill in the same proportion as the Westerners, it would have barely passed in the Senate and would have been defeated in the House by a substantial majority. Likewise, most other bills involving foreign policy have become laws because of overwhelming southern support. Did this southern belligerency indicate wholesale conversion to the establishment of the "Four Freedoms" everywhere? This question raises many others, which are not answerable until a time more calm and propitious to the researches of the objective historian than is the spring of 1942. Meanwhile the historian of the present may hazard the guess that if the policies and events of the past decade eventuate in the termination of finance capitalism and imperialism in general and of southern colonialism in particular, it will not be recorded that the southern politicians of the thirties and forties "willed it that way."*

* Reprinted by permission from *The Journal of Southern History*, January, 1942. This paper was read as the presidential address before the Southern Historical Association in Atlanta, November 7, 1941. Because of the national emergency, certain sentences in the concluding portion of the essays have been omitted here. The essay in its entirety may be found in *The Journal of Southern History*, as cited above.

# Garner versus Kitchin: A Study of Craft & Statecraft

*ALEX MATHEWS ARNETT*
*Professor of History*

A FULLER AND MORE accurate statement of my subject would be: the struggle between John Nance Garner, undercover promoter of reaction, and Claude Kitchin, leader of the liberal element, for control of the Democratic forces in the House of Representatives during the first Congress of the Harding-Coolidge-Hoover regime (1921-1922).

It was during this period, as we all now know, that the Democratic Party sold itself to mammon. In the process John Nance Garner, following his usual strategy of working in the dark, was a far more important and more active factor than has been known to the public, or even to the historians. Meanwhile, Claude Kitchin, also in the background at the time, though not from his own choice, put up a courageous fight, mostly from a sick bed, to hold his party in line with the liberal principles and policies which he conceived to be its mission.

Kitchin, a Representative from North Carolina, it may be remembered, had become the dominant figure in the House of Representatives in 1915 as majority leader and chairman of the powerful Ways and Means committee. He retained these key positions until the Republicans came into the ascendancy in both houses in 1919, after which he was minority leader and ranking Democratic member of that committee until his death in 1923.[1]

Kitchin was the antithesis of Garner in many ways.

Honest, consistent, capable, and hard-working, Kitchin was always open and aboveboard. Though shamefully misrepresented and maligned by a hostile press, his position on every public question was readily ascertainable by those who had the will and the opportunity to find out. Garner, on the other hand, trimmed his sails to the prevailing winds. He was liberal only when liberalism paid political dividends. As to his position on any question, he usually said with a poker face, "I have no opinion," or, "I have nothing to say."[2]

Wrote George Milburn in *Harper's:* "It is unlikely that there is any man in public life today who has had as much written about him and as little told about him as John Nance Garner." He quoted a publicity director of the Democratic National Campaign headquarters in 1932: "It's a funny thing: here's a man who has been before the public for thirty years, and yet nobody don't know nothing about him."[3]

In his formal education, Garner reached only the fourth grade in primary school. Kitchin was a college graduate.[4] Most of our knowledge of Garner thus far is vague and circumstantial. His political activities were carried on mostly in the privacy of offices, cloak rooms, hotel rooms, and lobbies in conversations that were strictly "off the record."

Fortunately, however, in the papers of Claude Kitchin, now in the library of the University of North Carolina, is the behind-the-scenes story of Garner's secret machinations in one of the most critical periods of his own career and that of the Democratic Party—the first year or two of Hardingism. The letters and other documents in that collection are most revealing as to Garner's principles and tactics.

It so happened that during the greater part of 1921, while the resurgent Republicans were in control of all branches of the government for the first time since 1913, Kitchin was on sick leave at his home in Scotland Neck, North Carolina. This absence left him no contact with fellow members except through correspondence; and as the fight within the party grew more tense, this correspondence grew more heavy and more revealing. Then, too, his very able secretary, Mr. C. H. England, whom he trusted almost as an *alter ego*, was allowed the privileges of the floor, the cloak rooms, and even the caucus chambers; and he wrote full accounts of the happenings to Kitchin.

During Kitchin's absence Garner sought, with growing success, to gain control of the Democratic forces in the House and on the Ways and Means committee and to commit them largely to the reactionary policies of the dominant Republicans. Reaction seemed the order of the day, and Garner was evidently ready to fall in line. Such a course to Kitchin was dishonorable and abhorrent; furthermore it would lead to political disaster, for, as he saw it, the Democrats could never hope to cope with the Republicans for reactionary support. The only hope he saw for the party's maintaining any substantial support (at least outside the Solid South) was in maintaining what to him was its traditional position as the champion of the interests of the plain people. He knew, of course, that the party had always had its apostates and still had them, but he retained an abiding faith in its liberal mission.[5]

Because of his attractive, forthright, and affable personality, and his well-known ability, Kitchin seems to have been the most popular man in the House in his day. Until he lost his once vigorous health, he commanded the Democratic forces in the House with virtual solidarity, except on such occasions as when he dared oppose Wilson's war policies and was confronted with all the powerful forces which a then popular and resourceful administration could wield. He had also held the support of his party's members of the Ways and Means committee. Such support he still held until his absence during the late spring, summer, and fall of 1921. It was during this time that Garner got in his work.

Garner either strung along with the Republicans, occasionally fighting sham battles which they evidently did not take very seriously, or else sought compromises involving concessions which presumably would advance the interests of his own Texas constituents. His defection developed step by step as time went on, and it was some months before the Kitchin liberals became aware of its full import.

In the late months of the Wilson administration, the Republican majority in Congress sought the enactment of an extremely high "Emergency" Tariff measure. Garner's first reaction was to fight the entire measure and the principles upon which it stood. And in the fall of 1920 he made speeches to this effect on the floor of the House. But by January, 1921 (after the election results had become known and analyzed), he came to accept the principle of the bill and was willing to support it, with modifications, provided it offered protection to the products of "farm and ranch" along with those of factory. (Remember his own "farm and ranch" interests and those of his constituents.) This, of course, was quite opposed to the position of the Kitchin liberals. As Kitchin was there at the time to fight Garner's move, the liberal forces won the caucus vote, 77 to 29. But even the 29 indicated that Garner was gaining support for his new position.[6]

The only inkling of what was going on in the secret conclaves of the Democratic membership that got into the press was that there was a division, that so many voted each way, and that Kitchin led the larger group. So far as I have been able to find out, searching the files of such papers as the *New York Times*, neither the name of Garner nor his part in the intra-party fight was mentioned. So the public was none the wiser. Nor were the historians.

When time came for the Democrats of the Ways and Means committee to file their minority report, Garner and Crisp and apparently one or two others refused to sign it. This fact was also kept quiet. Garner shrewdly suggested that Kitchin alone sign "for the minority." And he did so.[7]

Was this an isolated defection on Garner's part, and

could he be trusted by the liberals on subsequent issues? How Kitchin felt about the question at the time is not revealed; but whether he thought he could trust Garner on the matter, whether he was too sick when he left Washington for Scotland Neck to worry himself with the matter, or for whatever reason, he left Garner as temporary ranking Democrat on the Ways and Means committee, to lead the fight against the Permanent Tariff bill.[8] How well did Garner handle it?

Representative Oldfield, a liberal Democrat, wrote Kitchin in July, 1921: "Jack made a mighty [something omitted], but the Republicans got after him on his emergency tariff vote and speech and of course it was a great hardship. I was really mighty sorry for Jack, sorry he had made such an awful blunder. It's too bad for both Jack and the party. . . ."[9]

A few days later came a more shocking report from Oldfield: "Have just returned from Garner's office where the Democrats of the Ways and Means committee had a conference. . . . Garner, Collier, Crisp, and Martin are in favor of repealing the excess profits tax. . . ."[10] This, of course, was a Republican proposition. Kitchin, it may be recalled, was the chief author and proponent of this measure and had the virtually solid support of his party delegation at the time that it was first adopted, during the first World War.

Kitchin replied to Oldfield: "I can say to you right now . . . that I am opposed to the repeal of the excess profits tax and, if I stand alone, I shall file a vigorous minority report showing that every Democrat or Republican who votes for it is standing for the corporate interests, whose stock-holders stayed at home, three thousand miles from danger, and plundered the people and the government to the extent of $50,000,000,000 profits from 1916 to the present time. . . . Now it is simply monstrous for a Democrat who claims to be for the people and with the people to join with the Republicans who are simply tools of the special interests to relieve these millionaired corporate plunderers of taxes and put it elsewhere upon the people, especially when the Republican House has just passed a tariff bill which enables these same corporations to plunder the people an extra $5,000,000,000 a year. . . .

"Don't let our Democrats throw away our position of being with the people and against the special interests by surrendering absolutely to the propaganda that is being prosecuted throughout the country for the past two years. . . .

"I am afraid our Democrats are being intimidated by the propaganda. . . . If we surrender to it we might as well not make a fight in 1924. We will have no issue with the Republicans."[11]

In the next few days the correspondence makes it clear that Garner was forming a sort of cabal to string along with, or to compromise with, the Republicans on other important issues. For the excess profits tax, which exempted corporations making no more than 7 to 9 per cent and taxed on a graduated scale profits in the upper brackets, Garner and his group were willing to accept the Republican proposition of a flat 15 (later made 12½) per cent tax on all corporate profits regardless of their smallness or hugeness. Furthermore, he and his group were willing to make generous compromises with the Republican demand for drastic reductions on the income surtaxes, mainly in the higher brackets. This to "liberate more capital for investment"—one reason, by the way, for the runaway inflation that developed thereafter.[12]

Later in July (all dates from here on are for 1921 unless otherwise stated), Oldfield wrote Kitchin asking him to prepare "vigorous" minority reports on these questions, and meanwhile to send a telegram to be used among those members who might be influenced by his position and leadership as against Garner's. This he did. Oldfield wrote him a few days later that the telegram "stirred things up, . . . stiffened a good many, and was a solar plexus to Judge Garner . . .

and the like. . . ." He said further that in the fight on the Permanent Tariff Garner had again gone over to the protectionists, at least in large measure, in consideration for the inclusion on the highly protected list of hides, cotton, oil, and "other products of farm and ranch."[13]

A few days later Kitchin's secretary, England, wrote him with reference to Garner: ". . . he is the shrewdest, most cunning and enticing on the [Ways and Means] Committee, and he took it for granted . . . that you had gone home and would probably get out of touch with things here."[14]

Kitchin wrote Finis Garrett, another liberal on the Ways and Means committee, with reference to pending tax measures. ". . . I fear, however, our Democrats on the committee, some of them at least, headed by Garner, are going to throw away our whole position we have taken with the people by their going with the Republicans. . . . This is an absolute repudiation of the policy and abandonment of the fundamental principles of the Democratic party—that those most able to pay should pay more and those least able to pay should pay less. . . ."[15]

To Representative Collier, who had formerly been among the Kitchin group but who had gone over to Garner, Kitchin wrote: "For God's sake don't let Democrats like you be caught in the Republican net. . . ."[16]

Kitchin and his liberal following held that war taxes should not be materially reduced until the war debt was paid. Had their position prevailed, the inflation of the twenties would have been less extreme and probably the depression of the thirties less severe. Besides, we might have entered the depression with little or no Federal debt, in which case our present Federal debt would be very much less than it is.

Letters from liberal members and from Mr. England during early August revealed that Garner had persuaded nearly half the Democratic members of the Ways and Means committee not to sign Kitchin's minority report. Then the question arose whether it should go in with only his signature, as had been done in the case of the report on the Emergency Tariff, or whether the renegades should be brought into the open by the absence of only their signatures. The liberal members, even Oldfield, felt that it should not leak out to the public that the minority group was so badly divided. If it did, then much of the above-described behind-the-scenes dissension might leak out.[17]

Kitchin strongly favored a showdown. He wrote Oldfield insisting that all who were willing to sign his minority report do so, and not let it go in with only his signature. Referring to the latter course he wrote: "*This is what Garner wants.*"[18]

Faced with a possible showdown, Garner seemed to weaken for a time. Oldfield wrote Kitchin: "Jack Garner started out just as I wrote you in favor of the repeal of the excess profits tax and reduction of surtaxes and had Collier, Crisp, and Martin with him. However, Garner has weakened somewhat . . ."; also Crisp and Collier. Oldfield said he did not believe they had the nerve to face the issue publicly.[19]

Garner may have weakened momentarily; but England wrote Kitchin of a stormy conference in which Garner, Crisp, and some other Democratic members of the committee came into Kitchin's office to "have it out." There was a hot controversy. "Garner was all colors of the rainbow and some others."[20]

In the end, with all the uncertainties involved, it was the Oldfield group that weakened, and the report went in with only Kitchin's signature. Skeletons were again kept in the closet. The *New York Times's* report of the matter implied no suspicion as to the real significance of the solitary signature. It stated that such had happened before. Apparently it was merely a matter of convenience, Kitchin being absent and alone.[21]

Meanwhile the question arose as to whether the Democrats of the House should vote to recommit the entire tax revision bill on such grounds as Kitchin outlined. England wrote Kitchin: "Of all things imaginable that would nauseate, dishearten, and disgust has been the idiotic burlesque engaged in by the Democrats here for the last several days. Confidentially, I tried Judge Oldfield making a poll of the House [Democrats] and see if he could carry on a motion to recommit. . . . After the poll he said Garner would beat him three to one." Referring to the House Democratic caucus of the night before, England mentioned Crisp as "a noticeable rival of Garner's in rascality."[22]

The Democratic caucus the following day was stormy. The Kitchin forces, lacking the strength of his presence, went down to defeat. For the first time, Garner carried a substantial majority. Accounts of the struggle and the record vote are in the Kitchin collection, but not in the files of the newspapers or in the history books.

"Well," wrote Oldfield, "the fight is over, and Garner and his crowd have beaten us. . . . If you could have been here to lead the fight we would have won . . . Claude, the mistake we made was in not making the fight after the emergency tariff bill to remove Garner, Crisp, and Martin from the Committee. We could have won then. I believe we can win yet when you get able to take charge of the fight. The fact that John Garner is the ranking Democrat on the Committee when you are away gives the opposition [evidently referring to the Garner faction] a great advantage. . . .

"However," Oldfield added significantly, "it seems that the papers have not found out there has been a split. That is one good thing. . . ."[23] England also refers to this fact, adding with evident regret that this was just what Garner wanted; it gave him a chance to continue his work in the dark.[24]

Many were the letters that Kitchin received from members of his own forces lamenting the fact that he was not there to lead them in these crises. "If you were only here.

. . . " "If you could only have been here . . . ," they said. One of these is worth quoting further. It is from Representative A. R. Canfield:

"It is my personal view that at no time during your extended and distinguished service were you more needed in the House than now. Concurring in your view that certain members occupying prominent positions in the party lines are more interested in the welfare of special interests than in the mission of the Democratic party, I am entirely convinced that it is an hour when the really honest and progressive membership of the House minority should not only thoroughly exert itself but also let the country know the absolute position of the party." He deplored the fact that increasing numbers of Democrats were working with the Republican reactionaries.[25]

In October, 1922, after the storm had somewhat subsided, Garner wrote Kitchin:

"Of course differences will sometimes come up among us Democrats as to what to do, as it did in the Internal Revenue and the Tariff, but men like you and me, whose heart and conscience are with the great masses of the people, and who want to do what is best for the party, and thereby serve the country, never have any sore spots. . . ." He claimed to have been with Kitchin in principle all the time; they only differed in matters of detail.[26] Considering the great importance of the measures on which they differed, and the fundamental effects of Garner's policies in shaping the very character of the Democratic party then and for years thereafter, the least we can say of this conciliatory move is that it does not ring true. There seems to have been no reply.

Unfortunately Kitchin never regained his health to the point of being able to resume his active on-the-scene leadership. In the sadly thinning correspondence of his last months we find him still with the will to fight for his liberal principles and policies, but lacking in the physical power to make his fight effective in stemming the tide toward Garnerism.

The result was just as Kitchin, Oldfield, and others of their group had feared that it would be. The Democratic party surrendered its liberal position and became tweedle-dum and tweedle-dee with the Republicans. It thus became a pitiful minority and remained so until the frightful collapse of the Harding-Coolidge-Hoover Reign of Big Business and the resurgence of liberalism in a chastened and more or less regenerated Democracy under the leadership of Franklin D. Roosevelt.

Kitchin did score one last triumph before he died. He persuaded the Democratic caucus to disregard the seniority precedent and make Finis Garrett, who had been a consistent liberal, his successor as minority leader, instead of Garner, who was the ranking Democrat.[27] If this victory turned out to be rather futile, at least it must have given some satisfaction to Kitchin in his last days.*

* A paper delivered at the annual meeting of the Southern Historical Association in Atlanta, Georgia, November 6, 1941.

# The Economic Future of the Southeast

*ALBERT S. KEISTER*
*Chairman of the Department of Economics*

## CHARACTERISTICS OF THE SOUTHEAST

THE SOUTHEAST, despite its many fine qualities, is probably farther from an ideal democracy than any other region in the United States. Of all the regions, the Southeast has the lowest percentage of adult citizens participating in elections, clear evidence of a lack of political democracy. It has the lowest per capita incomes, the most malnutrition, the poorest paid farmers and wage workers, the most tenancy, the least unionization, all clear evidences of dire economic inequality and lack of economic democracy. This region also has the highest proportion of Negroes, involved, together with the poorer whites, in an informal caste system which makes southern society the antithesis of a social democracy. A frank facing of these facts is a necessary prerequisite to action. And action there must be, not only for the sake of the Southeast but for the sake of America as well. A weak region weakens the nation as a whole. National unity and strength, required not only for war times but also for the ominously threatening post-war world, demand that sore spots be made well.*

* The Southeast is not a clearly defined region. Its boundaries vary with different writers, with different administrative agencies of government, and with other groups dealing with regional problems. Roughly it corresponds with "The Old South," as distinguished from the newer Southwest. It usually includes the states of Virginia, North and South Carolina, Georgia, Florida, Alabama, Tennessee, and Mississippi. Sometimes included and sometimes not are the border states of Maryland, Kentucky, Arkansas, and Louisiana. In this essay the term is understood to mean the eight states first named and not the four border states, although the conditions analyzed and the conclusions reached may apply about equally well to the border states.

What kind of region is the Southeast? From the economic point of view, there are five outstanding characteristics of the region:

1. *The low average income of the people.*—The per capita income of the residents of this region in 1939 was estimated by the United States Department of Commerce to be $300. This compares with $537 for the average American, or a regional income only 56 per cent of the national average. Within the region the lowest incomes were in Mississippi, $203, and the highest in Florida, $457. A per capita regional income of $300 means an average family income of about $1200 to $1300 per year, as against approximately $2400 for the average American family. Since these figures are the *average*, they mean that a great many families, probably a considerable majority, received less than that sum.[1]

2. *The predominance of agriculture as an occupation.*—The Census of 1940 showed that 43.5 per cent of the people of this region live on farms, compared to 23 per cent in the nation at large.[2] As a means of support, the people of this region depend on agriculture to almost twice the extent that the American people as a whole do. Within the region the states with the highest proportions of people on farms are the states with the lowest per capita income. (See Tables in footnotes 2 and 3.) The two are clearly related. The more people in agriculture, particularly the kind of agriculture that prevails in the region, the lower the average income of all of the people in any one state in the region.

3. *The wide prevalence of tenancy in agriculture.*—More than half of the farmers in the Southeast own no land of their own (about 53 per cent tenants, 47 per cent farm owners in 1940). A large proportion of the tenants are share croppers, the lowest form of tenancy. The typical southeastern tenant farmer is characterized by frequent movings, indifference to the preservation of soil fertility, carelessness regarding buildings and equipment, and failure to raise a

garden and livestock. The system tends, therefore, to deplete the soil, yield poor crops, underfeed the people, and make agriculture unprofitable for both the tenant and the owner.

4. *The large proportion of Negroes in the population.*—The Southeast was the stronghold of slavery. It has been from colonial days, and still remains, the home of the American Negro. Over half of all the Negroes in America live in these eight states. The Negro has always been predominantly a worker on the land. He is the biggest factor in the tenancy problem. While his progress since 1865 has been noteworthy in many respects, he still constitutes a serious adjustment problem and especially so in this region.

5. *The highest birth rate in the nation.*—The Southeast has been called the seedbed of the nation because it is furnishing proportionally more of the children of America than any other region. For many years the birth rates in the Southeast have been the highest in the nation. In 1938, for example, the birth rate in the United States was 17.6. In every state in the Southeast the birth rate was above the national average, running from 18.5 in Tennessee to 26.5 in Mississippi.[3] Can America develop her highest power if she recruits her future citizens largely from the region where the incomes are the lowest?

These characteristics paint a dark picture. There is a brighter side, to be sure. Fine, hospitable people dwelling in one of the best climates in the world; a leisurely pace, giving time for fun and friendliness; recreation invited by accessible mountains, lakes, ocean, and Gulf; some excellent natural resources; inspiring achievements of the Tennessee Valley Authority; industries coming in; numerous signs of a determination on the part of the people to improve their schools, their homes, their diet, their government. The effort here is not to overlook nor to conceal the good. It is rather to analyze why we are where we are and what must be done to improve our status.

## WHY THE SOUTHEAST IS POOR

The fundamental difficulty with the Southeast is the imbalance between people and resources. There are too many people for the existing resources to support decently, under the present methods of using resources. We have about 12 per cent of the land area of the United States, while our population is about 16 per cent of the nation. This shows a density of population considerably above the American average. But with a large proportion of our land incapable of supporting many people well, because it is mountainous or heavily forested or swampy or badly eroded, the actual situation is worse than the figures suggest. If a large proportion of our people were engaged in manufacturing and other urban employment, an above-average density of population would be nothing to worry about. But many people scattered on poor land spells poverty, with all that the word poverty conveys in rural areas. Too many small farmers are spending their meager energy in growing cash crops for other markets, at the sacrifice of producing an adequate diet for themselves. The tragedy of the so-called "cash crops" is that little cash settles into the pocket of the farmer when the crop is sold and the bills are paid. Poor land and poor people! The relationship is reflected in the whole social and economic fabric of the region, and, in last analysis, of the entire nation.

Why is the Southeast so predominantly agricultural? Why has it not become industrialized, as New England and the other older regions have? Is it because of the machinations of northern capitalists, or the inherent shiftlessness of the Southerner, or the ruthlessness of General Sherman? None of these explains it. The entire story would be an intricate web of forces and factors working together. Only a few of the answers can be offered here.

Probably the chief reason is that throughout the greater part of the nineteenth century the staple crops of cotton and tobacco, especially the former, were so profitable as to attract our resources largely into their cultivation. We developed a "cotton economy," because on the whole it was highly profitable. It was heavily based on the labor of the black man, which was cheap and, when combined with good soil and climate, efficient enough to produce for most landowners a more generous return on their investment than could be obtained in any other form. Around cotton there developed a periphery of small businesses, such as gin operation, cottonseed oil and meal processing, warehousing and shipping, which depended upon and added to the strength of the cotton economy. This strength was not only economic but also social and political. The South became the stronghold of the free-trade and low-tariff sentiment of the country largely because the cotton planters dominated the South; and they sold in a free-trade, international market and wanted to buy in a similar one. Furthermore, a plantation economy is not friendly, socially or economically, to a manufacturing and industrial economy. Their ways of life are different, if not antagonistic. This does not mean that handicrafts and small manufacturers may not flourish alongside the plantation. They usually do, either as a subordinate part of the plantation itself or as near-by separate enterprises, dependent on the plantation to buy their product. Neither offers a threat to the domination of the planter; indeed they may contribute to it.

Closely related to the cotton economy as a reason for the slow development of manufacturing in the Southeast is another factor already mentioned, namely, the presence of a large majority of all the Negroes in America. Whether the Negro can develop high manufacturing and mechanical skills we do not know. We do know that he has not been given the chance and, unless racial barriers come down, is not going to be given the chance, in the near future at least. Manufacturing entrepreneurs, looking into the region and seeing a large proportion of the potential labor force excluded from consideration as mechanical employees and, in addition, because of low incomes, offering manufacturers almost no market for their products, may be forgiven for not having flocked in.

Another factor, also connected with the cotton economy, explaining our slower industrialization is our regional topography, especially the location of our mountains. Where the mountains come down close to the ocean, as in New England, agriculture sooner or later becomes impossible as the sole or even the chief means of support of the people. Either a break-through to more and better lands or the development of other means of livelihood must occur. In the Northeast both did occur, and the development of manufacturing and trade was one result. In the Southeast the mountains are hundreds of miles back from the ocean in the Carolinas and Georgia and practically disappear in northern Alabama. The result was to allow population to spread out and to remain agricultural. It is perhaps significant in this same connection to point out that a large part of whatever manufacturing has developed in the Southeast has done so in the Piedmont, where the hills and mountains made a barrier to further migration, discouraged agriculture by poorer soils, and offered water power for industrial development.[4]

The topography exercised a retarding influence on our industrial growth in another way. The mountains, being hundreds of miles back from the coast and being the highest in eastern North America, caused the early railroads into and out of this region to be built predominantly north and south, rather than east and west. Since the region to the north of us was the first in the country to be industrialized, and railroads offered cheap transportation, the Southeast came to depend on the Northeast for its manufactured goods, while it became a raw material producing region. After the freight rate structure solidified, it became very difficult to get rates favorable to the growth of manufacturing in this region. In the Gulf region, where the mountains were no barrier to east-west railroad building, opportunity did not beckon since settlement westward along the Gulf was scant and in that region the Mississippi River dominated the trade routes.

Another factor in our slow industrial development was the absence of the fertilizing effect of European immigration in the nineteenth century. While much of this immigration was of rural people who proceeded to a rural life in the Middle West, much of it was artisan in character and remained in the East as factory labor. Yankee ingenuity and inventiveness, the technological basis of northern industry, were largely the product of a favorable environment plus an artisan people. The South, because of its cotton economy, slavery and its aftermath, and lacking the mixture of artisan Europeans, failed to develop extensively the technical arts.[5]

One other factor may be mentioned. Manufacturing in the nineteenth century changed from its literal meaning of "making by hand" to its present meaning of "making by machinery." Manufacturing has become practically synonymous with machine industry. Today machine industry is largely refined combinations of coal and iron and oil. The most extensive early developments of these three essential resources were in the North, especially in Pennsylvania and later in the Great Lakes region. The basic iron and steel industry drew to itself many other industries, such as machinery manufacturing, machine tools, steel products of many kinds, and later the giant automobile industry. Each of these in turn has its satellite industries, buying from or selling to their main or central industry. All of these, together with an elaborate network of power and transportation agencies and serviced by banks, commercial and trade establishments, storage and shipping facilities, make a modern industrial region. But the fundamental basis is in coal, iron, and oil, particularly coal and iron, since they are not as easily and cheaply moved as oil. As a region the Southeast its largely lacking in these three basic essential resources. Only the Birmingham area offers extensive deposits of coal and iron. While this area shows promise of considerable future development, it labors under the handicaps of a late start and the lack of a highly developed, industrial hinterland.[6]

## THE CRISIS IN AGRICULTURE

Such are the major reasons for our slower industrialization. Our economy remains dominated by cotton. And it is this crop—cotton—that has encountered two crises recently. One is the serious decline in our export trade in cotton, due chiefly to the development of cotton raising in other parts of the world. The second is the rise of Texas as the leading cotton growing state. If large quantities are considered, cotton can be grown more cheaply in Texas than anywhere else in this country, with the possible exception of the Mississippi delta.[7] This means that in the long run, and not too long at that, the cultivation of short and medium staple cotton is going to shift from the older Southeast to the younger Southwest. This shift will not come over night. For many years the Southeast will continue to grow cotton, but on a diminishing scale. In short, world conditions are forcing America to raise less cotton. American conditions are forcing the Southeast to raise less of that lesser amount. The current rise in cotton prices, brought about by the war and government controls, promises to be only temporary and should not blind us to the fact that long-run trends spell less cotton culture in the United States and especially less in the Southeast.

What is true of cotton is true to a less degree of tobacco, the other main cash crop of the region. Tobacco is also suffering from reduced market outlets. It is more soil depleting than cotton. It works its farm families even more months in the year than cotton. It takes more commercial fertilizer than cotton; this means cash outlays from farmers whose cash incomes on the whole are small.

One of the basic causes, therefore, of the poverty of the Southeast is its lack of diversified farming. It has concentrated on a few cash crops to be sold in fluctuating and uncertain markets. It has not practiced proper crop rotation, especially with legumes and other soil-building plants. It has not had enough gardens, cows, pigs, and chickens. It lacks adequate capital to install up-to-date equipment. Its tenancy arrangements are too informal and temporary, offering no inducement for a tenant to build up the land and make one farm his home. It lacks experience with livestock and feed enterprises. Under present methods of cultivation its farms are too small to support their human partners adequately (the average southeastern farm is 81 acres of which only 28 are under cultivation). Much of the cultivated land is unfit for cultivation; it should be planted to trees or pasture. About one-half the land is eroded more or less badly—worst in the Piedmont. In 1940 the average American farmer got more income from livestock than from crops. Not so the southeastern farmer. The census figures are:

SOURCES OF GROSS FARM INCOME DOLLAR, 1940

| | From Crops | From Livestock and Livestock Products | From Government Payments | Total |
|---|---|---|---|---|
| United States | .38 | .54 | .08 | 1.00 |
| Southeastern Region | .57 | .34 | .09 | 1.00 |
| Alabama | .49 | .36 | .15 | 1.00 |
| Florida | .76 | .21 | .03 | 1.00 |
| Georgia | .58 | .31 | .11 | 1.00 |
| Mississippi | .54 | .28 | .18 | 1.00 |
| North Carolina | .67 | .28 | .05 | 1.00 |
| South Carolina | .62 | .27 | .11 | 1.00 |
| Tennessee | .45 | .47 | .08 | 1.00 |
| Virginia | .48 | .50 | .02 | 1.00 |

Whereas the average American farmer received 54 cents out of every dollar from livestock and livestock products, the southeastern farmer received only 34 cents from that source. Only in Tennessee and Virginia, among the region's eight states, did the farmers get more income from livestock than from crops, but neither of those states was up to the national average. Through livestock and its products, a farmer's corn and hay and other crops can usually be marketed more profitably than as crops. In addition, livestock enriches the soil and gives the farm family a better diet. One important answer to the plight of agriculture in this region is more livestock and what accompanies it—meat packing, butter, cheese, eggs, milk. Two of the chief obstacles to greater cattle production, the cattle tick and the absence of good native pasture grasses, must be overcome.

What evidences are there that agriculture is changing for the better? The 1940 Census of Agriculture offers some encouraging answers. During the ten years from 1930 to 1940, while the total population of the region was increasing 11 per cent, the farm population increased only 2 per cent, showing that migration from the farms was relieving the pressure on the land somewhat. The number of farms decreased 6 per cent, while the average farm increased in size 17 per cent, promising a more adequate base for the average farm family to work on. The number of farm owners increased 10 per cent, while the number of tenants decreased 17 per cent, an encouraging trend away from tenancy. The number of cattle on farms increased 31 per cent, the gallons of milk produced increased 29 per cent, the number of hogs increased 45 per cent, tons of hay produced increased 60 per cent, while the number of bales of cotton raised decreased 26 per cent. The average farm is valued at about $30 per acre, a figure which means that the price of land is not a serious deterrent to the purchase of a farm. Besides the official census figures, there is encouragement in some things seen by travellers through the region—the terracing, the contour plowing, the stands of legumes, notably kudzu and lespedeza, the pine seedlings on eroded hillsides, the permanent pastures.

The domination of this region by agriculture spreads its influence beyond mere farming. Life in the region has an agrarian tone. The state legislatures are almost uniformly dominated by the agricultural segment of the population and its point of view, with results clearly apparent in the statutes enacted, including revenue and appropriation measures. The attitudes toward education, toward Negroes, toward the church and religion and the Bible, toward strangers and hospitality, toward social and economic changes, all reflect more an agricultural than an industrial philosophy of life.

### FOREST RESOURCES

Closely associated with agriculture is forestry. Over half of all the land in the Southeast is in forests. This region has always been one of the major sources of American lumber supplies. It still is. The typical farmer looks to his wood lot for supplemental income. Many of them work for local sawmills. Neat piles of pulpwood by the roadside testify to an important use of forest products. More than half of all of the rosin and turpentine produced in America comes from the trees in this region. Furniture factories have long been here, paper mills are steadily increasing, both based on the forests. Add to these economic aspects of forests the other benefits of woodlands—the beauty, the recreational advantages, the wild-life refuges, the conservation possibilities—and one gains some appreciation of the importance of this oft-forgotten resource.

About 5 per cent of the forest land in the Southeast is owned by the public. The other 95 per cent is owned about half and half by farmers and private corporations.[8] Best cared for are the public forests; next best are those owned in large tracts by commercial companies, interested in future supplies of timber to feed their plants or to furnish lumber for the American market; least well cared for are the forests owned by farmers. Fires are the greatest enemy of our forests. More fires are caused by incendiaries than by any other factor. Some cattle owners in open range country are known to start extensive forest fires in order to increase the stand of grass. Most farmers do not look upon their woodlands as a permanent source of income. They take the short view, selling and cutting their best timber with little regard to other trees or to sound reforestation principles. Good forest management means careful planting and thinning, protection against fires and other enemies, and continuous selective cutting; the thinnings and culls sold for pulpwood, the mature trees for lumber. Nature, with her abundant rainfall and long growing season, offers ideal conditions for tree growth in this region. Wood is the raw material for an expanding array of industries in the modern world—pulp, paper, paper board, rayon, furniture, synthetic products based on cellulose, to mention only a few. The Southeast has an inviting future as one of the main sources of America's

AN ECONOMIC VIEW OF THE SOUTHEASTERN REGION AND ITS CHIEF NEEDS, IN BROAD OUTLINE

I. WHAT THE REGION HAS NOW

| AGRICULTURE | | | | INDUSTRY | |
|---|---|---|---|---|---|
| Chief Source of Income, Farming | Secondary Sources of Income | | | Peace Time Industries | Defense Industries |
| | *Forests on Farms* | *Crafts on Farms* | *Jobs near Farms for Farm People* | | |
| Crops, livestock, dairy products, etc., for market and for own use. | Timber used on farm and sold in market. | Bedspreads, pottery, care of tourists, etc. | Road work, saw mills, fruit and vegetable packing, odd jobs in town, etc. | Factories, mines, lumbering, fishing, resort hotels and beaches, stores, shops, service industries, professional lines, government work, etc. | Training camps<br>Naval and air bases<br>Manufacturing plants<br>Shipbuilding |

II. THE REGION'S CHIEF NEEDS

| AGRICULTURE | | | | INDUSTRY | |
|---|---|---|---|---|---|
| Chief Sources of Income, Farming | Secondary Sources of Income | | | Peace Time Industries | Defense Industries |
| | *Forests on Farms* | *Crafts on Farms* | *Jobs near Farms for Farm People* | | |
| Migration from the farms. Improved farm practices. More livestock, food, and feed crops. Soil rebuilding and conservation. Co-operatives. Better tenant leases, etc. | Better management to gain and conserve long-term income. | General development. Improved marketing. Tourist housing regulations. | More of the desirable kinds. | Expansion, especially of the desirable kinds that will create jobs and balance the present economy. | Planning for post-defense readjustments. |

supply of wood. We can provide that future supply of wood largely from land that is good for nothing else. At the same time we can control much of the erosion that is carrying away our top soil, prevent floods, conserve our water supplies, protect game, fish, and other wild life and make the region attractive to campers, tourists, and recreation seekers.

## WHAT THE REGION IS AND WHAT IT NEEDS

Before taking up industry, it may prove helpful to have a brief, over-all view of the problem. In outline form it appears on page 160. The outline oversimplifies the existing economy, in that everything is reduced to the two headings —Agriculture and Industry. Under each of these headings numerous features could not be included. The attempt is merely to sketch in broad terms what the region has now to build on and what its chief needs are.

It will be noted that Agriculture is a larger block than Industry, since the former provides a livelihood for considerably more of our people than the latter. Farmers obtain their chief income from farming, though the secondary sources of income are significant and promise to be more so as time goes on. Industry is subdivided into peace-time and defense industries, a classification clearly pertinent to present conditions but, we may hope, of doubtful long-term validity. The items under "The Region's Chief Needs" call for only a few words of explanation. Migration from the farms is necessary to relieve the overpopulation now pressing on the land. This migration should be in part to places outside of the region where employment opportunities are inviting. It should be in part to places, especially towns and cities, within the region where, as new industries are established and old ones expand, jobs are created. This means that man power will be shifted from the agricultural sector to the industrial for the benefit of both. A declining birth rate is also needed in the region to synchronize with industrial expansion, the two working together in the long run to relieve the pressure of population on the land and to raise the standard of living.

### MORE INDUSTRIES NEEDED

The chief hope of economic betterment in the Southeast lies in an increased tempo of industrialization. This assumes that the philosophy of the agrarians is not destined to dominate the future policy. If the policy is to thwart industrialization and insist upon an agrarian future, it is difficult to see how the region can escape widespread starvation, since there is not room enough on the land for all of our present population, and the pressure will be considerably greater in another generation. Only by extensive migration or a completely revolutionized agriculture could the calamity be avoided. Extensive migration would mean that industry in other parts of the country would be expected to absorb our surplus people, a solution hardly consistent with an agrarian philosophy. A revolutionized agriculture, sufficiently thoroughgoing to support our present and prospective numbers, would completely alter the whole pattern of southern life, substituting a kind of European peasantry for what we have now. This is so completely alien to our traditions and way of life that it may be dismissed from present consideration.

What are the prospects for further and rapid industrialization? What industries may we reasonably expect to draw? To what extent must we mortgage our future to northern capital to obtain new industries? What hopeful and what discouraging signs of industrial growth are visible on the horizon?

First of all, the two types of industry pertinent to this discussion should be distinguished. One is the manufacturing industry; the other is what may be called the service industry. The former is illustrated by the new plant, bringing jobs and payrolls and increased population and purchasing power to a local community. The other includes the various businesses or industries that automatically follow the first—the bakeries, the ice cream plants, the garages, the stores, the filling stations, the laundries and dry cleaning plants, all that array of service establishments that spring up as a community is able to support them. This second type need not be gone after. It will come if the first type comes. A new manufacturing plant, therefore, creates jobs directly within itself; it also creates jobs indirectly through the additional community facilities needed by the increased local population. The key to increased industrialization and job creation is therefore additional *manufacturing* plants.

While the Southeast has been handicapped by a late start in the manufacturing game, it has made more progress in the past forty years than America as a whole has made. The late start is due to the fact that while the Northeast was establishing firmly its manufacturing leadership, notably during the generation from 1840 to 1880, this region was absorbed in the slavery and reconstruction issues. By the time the environment became peaceful and settled, favorable to capital investment and industrialization, the region was considerably behind the procession. The rate at which it has been catching up, however, is encouraging. During the forty years from 1899 to 1939 the successive censuses of manufactures show that manufacturing in this region has grown at a faster rate than in the nation as a whole.[9] The number of wage earners employed in factories in the region has increased 141 per cent, while the increase in the nation at large has been 75 per cent. Wages paid in the region have increased sixfold as against a fourfold increase in the country as a whole. The value of products manufactured in the region was nine times as great in 1939 as in 1899, whereas in the entire country the value was five times as great. On the fourth test, value added by manufacture, which is the difference between the value of the raw materials and the value of the final finished product, the region showed a 700 per cent gain as against 430 per cent in the country as a whole.[10]

The figures also reveal some conditions not so bright. In

1939 this region had 13 per cent of the nation's wage earners but they received only 8.5 per cent of the nation's wages. The wages per worker in the region for that year were about $750, whereas in the nation as a whole they were about $1,150. There are four principal reasons why our industrial workers get so much lower wages than the average American. One is the oversupply of labor in the region, a condition which always has a depressing effect on wages. A second is that the workers lack high skills, the great majority being in the unskilled and semi-skilled categories rather than in the skilled. This is partly due to lack of mechanical training in the educational system and partly to the low skill requirements of most of the regional industries. The third reason is the lag in the development of labor organization in the region. The fourth is that a large proportion of the manufacturing plants are engaged in the making of low-value products, a situation which in turn makes the paying of high wages difficult or impossible. It is a noteworthy fact that much of the manufacturing of the Southeast consists of taking raw products through the first stages of processing only. Sawmills, planing mills, cotton spinning and weaving, and fertilizers are prominent examples of this type of industry and they employ a large number of wage earners. If other "first process" employments more closely related to agriculture were included, such as lumbering, turpentining, cotton ginning, and cottonseed oil and meal processing, the proof would be even more emphatic that the industries of the Southeast are very largely occupied with working raw products through the early stages only. This is not profitable to labor, nor on the whole to employers, since such goods usually enter highly competitive markets where they sell for low prices and return meager rewards to the labor and capital employed. This process also means that many of these goods leave the region to be finished and are later brought back into the region to be consumed. Some of these advanced and finishing processes could and should be carried on profitably within the region. There are encouraging signs, particularly in the field of textiles, that more and more of the regional manufactures are being finished within the region or at least are being carried much farther than formerly toward the final consumers' goods stage. The future of the Southeast depends in part on the development of more industries making final consumers' goods and goods of higher unit value.

Of the one million industrial wage earners in the region, one half are working in textiles. It is *the* industry of the Southeast. Among the various textiles, cotton manufacturing is far more important than all the others, though rayon is growing rather rapidly. The cotton mills in this region spin and weave about 75 per cent of the American total. North Carolina leads all other states, using over two million bales annually or about 26 per cent of all the cotton processed in the nation.

The pattern of location of the cotton manufacturing industry in the Southeast differs strikingly from that in New England and the British Isles in its diffusion and decentralization. There is no textile center in the South comparable to Fall River, Massachusetts, or Manchester, England. Typically, the plants are in or near small cities, many of them being in the open country, surrounded by the mill village.* The mills are not, however, diffused uniformly over the Southeast but lie for the most part in the Piedmont in a broad crescent, running from Danville in southern Virginia to Montgomery, Alabama, in an area about one hundred miles wide.

Diffusion of the industry among many communities means that the typical mill is close to the farms, from which,

* Since many of the mills were built outside the towns, some one had to build houses and provide streets, water, and other utilities. The mill companies usually looked after these things and charged less than commercial rates for their use. Houses are rented typically for about one dollar per room per month. Part of the "real wages" of the workers have been paid in such forms. Critics have assailed the paternalism and control over private life involved in these arrangements, but in many cases they were necessary under the circumstances.

historically, nearly all of the labor has been recruited. There is considerable migration even today from farm to mill and back again. Agriculture in the Piedmont region has long suffered from overpopulation and eroded land. Employment in cotton mills has provided a needed escape for thousands of these farm families. When they move to mill villages, they usually come into contact with improved health facilities, better schools for their children, more social life, and certainly more money than they had possessed previously. With many of them mill employment also means irksome indoor work of a monotonous character, to which personal adjustment is difficult and in some cases impossible. The long hours, which formerly prevailed in many of the mills, with considerable night work and extensive employment of women and children, also complicated the problems of family adjustment in a new environment. There is no doubt that mill employment, especially when more than one member of the family worked, raised the *economic* status of the average family. Whether it meant an improvement in general contentment and satisfaction in life for the families involved is more doubtful.

While the processing of cotton through its early stages has been by far the leading industry and a source of much-needed employment in the region, it is not a satisfactory industrial base for the future. It carries too deeply the marks of a colonial economy—producing raw materials and then carrying them through the first processes of manufacture only. It does not create high values per worker or per dollar of capital invested. It cannot therefore pay high wages or make prosperous local communities.

In the development of textile industries the Southeast may be repeating the history of England and New England. There seems to be a well-developed tendency for a new textile region to start with the spinning and weaving processes, sending the gray goods out into the older regions to be dyed, finished, and made into final manufactured forms; then, for the dyeing and finishing industries to come in, seeking proximity to the weaving plants, followed by concerns manufacturing the coarser and cheaper grades of finished consumer and industrial goods. The last stage is the development of industries specializing on high-grade, high-value finished goods, with attendant satellite industries producing accessories and servicing the main plants. The last stage comes partly as a mere matter of age and maturity, and partly as skilled labor, markets, and capital facilities are developed. The Southeast is now in the intermediate stage, developing its dyeing, finishing, and coarse-goods manufacturing. If history repeats itself, the future will witness a regional growth in the manufacture of the finer grades of goods and the lines more profitable to the owners, the workers employed, and the states which protect them.

Next to the textile industries in regional importance come the wood industries. Over 150,000 people are employed in these industries, chiefly in sawmills, veneer mills, planing mills, pulp and paper mills, furniture plants, and plants making wooden boxes and paper board. Then follow food and feed products employing about 60,000 workers; tobacco manufactures employing about 33,000; iron and related products, concentrated chiefly around Birmingham and occupying some 30,000 wage earners; earthen products (brick and tile, lime, cement, concrete products, etc.), about 18,000 workers; and a considerable array of smaller miscellaneous industries.

## LOCATIONAL FACTORS

If increased industrialization is the chief need of the Southeast, it is relevant to inquire what the chief factors are that govern the location of new industries and what hope there is that these forces will pull additional industries to this region. The chief factors influencing the location of private industries are:

1. Natural resources and raw materials

2. Labor supply and labor costs
3. Markets
4. Fuel, power and transportation
5. Finance, especially capital supply and taxation conditions.

Space permits only a brief treatment of each of these factors. It is understood that private industries (in contrast to government industries) base their location decisions almost solely on cost and profit considerations. They are not in business primarily to help a region or a local community. In weighing the various location factors, a specific industry will usually find that some factors pull one way and others an opposite way. To be near their raw materials and a cheap labor supply the ladies' garment industry might be drawn to the Southeast, but markets and proximity to style centers might outweigh these factors and pull the industry to the New York area. Location decisions are usually compromises that attempt to combine the most advantages with the fewest disadvantages, reckoned from the cost of production standpoint.

1. *Natural resources and raw materials.*—Manufacturing industries experiencing a strong pull toward raw material sources are: (a) those in which the manufacturing process results in a great reduction of bulk, hence of transportation costs. Ore smelting is an example. Sawmills, citrus juice canning, and perhaps in the future, dehydration of vegetables are pertinent examples for this region; (b) those in which the raw material is highly perishable and must be processed close to its source for that reason. Fish packing, cheese making, fruit and vegetable canning illustrate this locational tendency; (c) those using the by-products of another industry. A large meat packing plant may have a number of by-product plants around it. Cottonseed oil plants are close to the cotton gins.

If the Southeast shifts the agricultural base of its economy from cotton to more food crops, livestock, and dairying, the change will mean fewer cottonseed oil mills but more creameries, cheese factories, and condensed milk plants; fewer cotton gins but more meat packing plants. Net employment will increase since the newer industries will use more labor than the old. More value will be added to the raw material; hence we may expect better wages, better returns to capital, better diets, sounder health, more revenues to the counties and states for improvements in schools and other public functions—altogether a desirable change.

2. *Labor supply and labor costs.*—A region characterized for generations by the highest birth rate in the nation with scant industrial opportunities for employment has meant "cheap labor and plenty of it." Despite migration the labor supply has been overabundant, depressing wage scales and living conditions and producing chronic unemployment and partial employment. Malnutrition has lowered efficiency and vitality; lack of vocational training has glutted the market for unskilled labor; the large proportion of Negroes in the labor force has further congested the unskilled ranks, forcing wages for both whites and blacks to low levels.

To what extent the large reservoir of under-employed labor in the region has attracted industry, it is impossible to say. Employers are not interested in wages as such. They are interested in labor costs. A skilled man at $10 a day may be cheaper than a bungler at $2 a day. Even though a firm is convinced that labor costs would be appreciably lower in Georgia than in Ohio, the saving in labor cost might be more than cancelled by the greater distance from the firm's markets, or from its sources of raw materials. Only if lower labor costs are not offset by other factors is there a pull toward a low labor cost region.

It is generally known that lower wages have been a potent factor in attracting the cotton textile industry to the Southeast. That the cotton mills in this region for many years paid lower hourly wages than those in New England, even allowing for mill-village housing and other forms of "wages in kind," is well established. These lower hourly rates of pay combined with the longer average work-week and fewer restrictions on night work prevailing in the southeastern states prior to the Federal codes of the 1930's unquestionably meant lower labor costs and, other things being equal, lower cost of producing yarn and cloth in the mills of this region.

Whether or not wages are at present a drawing card toward the Southeast is difficult to determine. As pointed out previously, the high birth rate and the impoverished agriculture of this region have produced an oversupply of unskilled labor. Nearly all of this unskilled labor can, with varying amounts of industrial training, be developed into semi-skilled labor. The large supply of labor in the region is, therefore, actually or potentially in the unskilled and semi-skilled ranks. In a free demand-supply market this would make for low wages, which would tend in turn to attract industries using relatively large amounts of these kinds of labor. But two forces are counteracting this pull. One is the Federal Fair Labor Standards Act, commonly known as the Wage-Hour Law. This statute is designed to elevate labor standards where they are abnormally or naturally low and bring them more nearly into conformity with the national average. The other force is the growth of unionization, which works toward the same end. These two forces, while raising the level of those employed, tend to retard the employment of those unemployed, through weakening the wage attractions of the region.

However, above the statutory level there is still room for wage and hour variations among regions and industries. It may also be noted that both the Wage-Hour Law and unionism failed to include or affect some industries. In these industries the lower wage level in the Southeast would still tend to exert some pull.[11]

It may be concluded that in our two leading industries, textiles and wood products, the wage factor has been an important locational element. Further development of these industries may be expected in this region not only on account of lower labor costs but also because raw materials and other factors combine to make location in this region attractive. The apparel and cast-iron industries also look promising for this region, since with them also both labor and raw material factors combine to point to the Southeast.[12]

3. *Markets.*—Because of the low incomes and the rural character of the great majority of our people, the Southeast does not offer attractive markets to most industries at present. With industrialization and rising incomes, the markets for consumer goods and services will expand and the service industries will expand correspondingly. The markets for business or producers' goods will likewise grow with industrialization and tend to attract satellite industries, clustering around main plants.

4. *Fuel, power, transportation.*—For most industries fuel, power, and transportation costs are minor elements, and hence not determinative of location. In fact, cheap electric power tends to decentralize industry, freeing it to locate on the basis of other factors. But with particular industries, one or more of these three factors may be so important as practically to determine location. The aluminum industry is anchored to cheap electric power. The iron smelting industry is drawn toward its fuel supply—coking coal. Cheap transportation facilities, such as by waterways, may attract industries having a heavy transportation burden. Oil refineries, for example, find economies in locations on the ocean and the Great Lakes, whence shipments can be made by tankers. Sugar refineries are frequently found in seaboard cities to take advantage of cheap ocean transportation.

The Southeast, with access to both the Gulf and the Atlantic, has cheap water transportation on two sides. This may prove an increasingly valuable asset as Central and South America develop. Unfortunately, the freight rate structure discriminates against this region. It must be altered to remove one of the handicaps of the Southeast.

5. *Finance, especially capital and taxation factors.*—

Most new industries nowadays do not base their location primarily on local capital supply. There are many communities with a surplus of capital while the banking and investment machinery designed to shift capital from place to place is well developed. This means that there is still enough "risk capital" in enough communities to allow most locational decisions to be made on other grounds than proximity to capital. True, some investors are more willing to "go in" if the enterprise will locate locally. Occasionally a local group organizes and finances a new enterprise expressly for the community. But if it is competitive with enterprises in other communities, it is likely to be short-lived unless other factors, such as materials, markets, and labor are favorable. Another condition tending to make capital considerations less potent in choosing location is that a large proportion of new factory capacity being built today consists of extensions or branch plants of existing corporations. The location of these new facilities is likely to be made on careful, rational bases. Capital supply is not even a minor factor.

While it is undoubtedly true that the Southeast has always been a debtor region, it does not follow that this has impoverished the region or kept it poor. Outside capital has permitted the development of resources earlier and more rapidly than if the region had depended on its own savings. Even granting that the profits were taken out of the region, there were substantial benefits left in the developed resources. To what extent the profits have really been taken out of the region, no one knows. It is true that many southeastern industries are partially or wholly owned by corporations domiciled in the North, but no one knows to what extent the stocks and bonds of these corporations are owned by residents of this region. It is known that northern life insurance companies lend large sums on mortgage security in this region, but it is not known to what extent that money has been supplied to those companies by southeastern policyholders. It is impossible to tell to what extent any region is, on net balance, a debtor or a creditor region.

This is not to argue that outside capital is better for a region than local capital. On the contrary, it would be decidedly advantageous for the region to develop its own capital resources extensively. Local ownership is better socially than absentee ownership. It is also better economically because the interest and the profits are retained to enrich the region. And there is some encouraging evidence that the region is increasing its liquid capital. Bank deposits, which are considered a good index of capital conditions, increased approximately 23 per cent between 1930 and 1940 in the region, as against 13 per cent in the nation at large.[13] It is safe to say that industrial development is not being held back in this region by lack of capital.

Some states and cities have tried to attract industries by tax concessions and other inducements, such as aid in building or equipping their plants. On the whole, these are probably unimportant and unsuccessful efforts, when it comes to attracting worth-while, permanent industries. An industry that will go to a state or community because it can save property taxes for a few years or avoid some capital investment in plant is putting secondary considerations first. Unless there are sounder reasons for such a location, the enterprise is not likely to be able to survive in competition with rivals in superior locations.

While governmental inducements are not likely to be effective in attracting to a region industries not suited to the region, they may be effective in drawing a plant to a particular state or city, if it is coming to the region anyway. If labor and other primary factors are approximately equal for a new hosiery mill in either North Carolina or Tennessee, tax concessions may swing the balance in favor of the state offering the concessions. Similarly with respect to county or town concessions within a state.

Taxation authorities are practically unanimous in condemning the practice of a state or a community offering tax concessions or other inducements to industry. Such concessions are at the expense of somebody, usually the other taxpayers including businesses already in the community. The new industry may force additional expenses on the municipality, such as new streets and schools to be built for the increased population. If it proves to be short-lived it may leave stranded families to be cared for by relief agencies. It is admitted that if the new industry would not have come otherwise and proves to be a strong, permanent addition to the economic life of the community, temporary tax concessions may be more than offset by gains in other directions. But few such cases are to be found. Generally speaking, the industries that are worth having must be won on other grounds than temporary governmental subsidies.[14]

## FACTORS FAVORABLE TO INDUSTRY

Toward the coming of needed industries, there are certain favoring pulls. Chief of these are:

1. *A population excess, making for low wages.*—The Southeast has the highest birth rates and, partly as a result, has the lowest average wages of all the regions of the United States. These conditions are attractive to certain industries, especially to those that are foot-loose and use relatively large amounts of unskilled and semi-skilled labor. A plentiful supply of cheap native labor may not reflect a desirable social condition but it may be one of the elements whereby that condition itself is improved.

2. *Raw materials and semi-processed goods available.*—The fact has already been noted that many of our industries, especially in textiles and wood products, process their materials through the early stages only. The finishing processes and the production of the final consumers' goods are carried on to a large extent in other regions. Where style factors are the governing element in location, this is rational. But the growth of textile finishing plants and of various forms of the clothing industry within the region shows that its textile industries are becoming better integrated and more fully rounded. In the field of wood products, the multiplication

of furniture and paper plants testifies to the same tendency. Similar developments may be under way in iron and steel, in food and feed products, in clay and pottery, in chemicals and tobacco. Wherever raw materials are a major factor in dedermining location, the abundance of certain materials in this region becomes a drawing card.

3. *Mild climate, making for lower operating and living costs.*—Where much outdoor work is involved or where mild weather is desired either for the material or the human factor to operate best, the Southeast has an attractive resource in its climate. The number of man-days per year lost on account of weather tie-ups, colds and other illness, and inability to get to work every day on time would doubtless be appreciably lower in the Southeast than in the North, if careful records were kept. Whether living costs are lower depends on what is being compared. Reports of the Bureau of Labor Statistics indicate that it costs the average southeastern family about as much as the average northern family to live, *if they buy the same things.* But they do not buy the same things. The southeastern family typically eats different foods (and cheaper ones), wears less clothing, uses less fuel, furniture, and medical service, and in general lives on a somewhat lower and less expensive plane than the northern. It has to because its income is lower. To some extent this lower actual cost of living is validated by the milder climate. Nature helps out in the family's living costs. This factor in turn affects wages, offering some basis for the argument that "a regional wage differential favoring the South is justified because it costs less to live in the South." Climatic advantages are also evident in the long growing season, considerable rainfall, and the out-of-door living possible for men and animals most of the year.

4. *The trend toward decentralization of industry.*—Progress in the technology of power production has loosened the hold of coal on industry location. When it required five pounds of coal to generate one kilowatt hour of electricity,

which was not so long ago, coal would move long distances only under exceptionally favorable circumstances. Industrial centers grew up around coal deposits. Today, with less than one pound of coal required to generate one kilowatt hour and with water power in some places capable of doing it even more cheaply than coal, most industry is no longer tied to coal. It is freer than formerly to locate where labor or market or other factors are favorable. Electricity, too, can be economically carried longer distances than a few years ago, which also tends to make industry more foot-loose. These decentralizing forces should be helpful in furthering the industrialization of the Southeast.

5. *Social trends.*—Certain broad social trends are favoring the industrial development of the Southeast. Public opinion has been aroused, both inside and outside of the region, regarding the problems of the region. The plight of cotton, the high farm tenancy ratio, the poverty, ill health, and malnutrition of the people, especially the rural people, have attracted the attention of the nation in recent years. Until defense became the main concern of the American people, "Economic Problem Number 1" was being increasingly thought about. To cure the plight of agriculture and the unemployment and under-employment resulting from excess population, increased industrialization has always been among the first remedies suggested. There was and still is unanimous agreement that the Southeast must have more manufacturing. Before defense intervened, steps were being taken to implement the conclusion. The freight rate structure was being attacked with some promise of success. Many communities in the Southeast were aroused to their own needs and were putting forth strenuous efforts (not always wise) to attract new industries. Capital has been steadily accumulating in the region, seeking investment. Industry has been expanding faster than in the nation at large. The establishment of the Tennessee Valley Authority was a dramatic move by the Federal government to improve condi-

tions in the region. All signs pointed to the conclusion that both the Southeast itself and the nation at large recognized the need for greater industrialization and were doing something about it. Whether the war will thwart these forces permanently or only temporarily remains to be seen. In some respects the defense effort itself has helped rather than hindered the trend toward industrialization. Not only have some large defense industries been located within the region but also an even larger proportion of training camps and air and naval bases. These defense centers train local labor in higher skills, enhance local trade by an increased volume of spending, and attract a large flow of visitors and tourists to the region, some of whom will remain to help build up the region in the future.

## FACTORS UNFAVORABLE TO INDUSTRY

In contrast to the favorable pulls, there are certain unfavorable factors which should be realistically faced. Chief of them are:

1. *Lack of rich, varied natural resources.*—The soil of the Southeast is on the whole not highly fertile, though the Mississippi delta and certain other areas are exceptionally good in this respect. Lush and nutritious pasture grasses, the base of a livestock and dairying industry, are not native and so far have been difficult to acclimate. Outside of the Birmingham area, there are few rich deposits of minerals which can be exploited commercially in competition with other regions. Manufacturers oriented on cheap and abundant raw materials do not find in the Southeast a wide variety of opportunities.

2. *Low incomes and poor markets.*—Manufacturers oriented on markets likewise find the region a handicap, inasmuch as the low buying power of the people causes weak regional markets. A vicious circle is apparent: lack of industrialization is largely responsible for low per capita income, which in turn make the region a poor market, which in turn

makes the region an unattractive location for industries oriented on the market.

3. *The freight rate structure.* The Southeast has long complained that the railroads have thwarted industrialization by discriminatory freight rates. That freight rates on many commodities between points in southern territory and points in official classification territory are higher than between points the same distance apart within official territory or between official and western territory is freely admitted. The justification offered by the railroads (greater density of traffic in official territory, etc.) is harder to appraise. Encouragement is already being found in recent acts of the Interstate Commerce Commission, in the growth of competing truck traffic, and in the development of inland waterways, notably the Tennessee River.

4. *An immature economy.*—New industries tend to go where older industries already are. There they are likely to find skilled labor, repair and service facilities, bankers familiar with their problems, transportation and communication systems, and numerous other environmental conditions favorable to the new establishments. Industry breeds industry. Age and experience count. As previously noted, the Southeast got a late start in manufacturing and still suffers from the handicap. The people are rural-minded, not industry-minded. Schools are poorly supported and offer for the most part a meager diet of elementals. Trade and technical training is rare. The people do not have the "feel" of the machine. Race prejudice is a barrier to free mobility of labor. When a new industry comes in, it must as a rule bring along its technicians and foremen, then train the local labor in the skills needed. Such an environment is unfavorable to many types of industry, especially to those making high-quality and high-value goods—the types that pay well to labor, to investors, and to the community at large. It will take time for the Southeast to develop industrial maturity.

## WHAT SHOULD BE DONE?

How shall the region proceed to get action to further desirable industrial trends? How can location policies be implemented? The answers must necessarily be along broad regional lines, not attempting to suggest how a particular community or even a state should proceed to get the particular industry or industries it needs.

Any action contemplated must be cognizant of the fact that future industrialization of this or any other region will be a balance between government policy and private enterprise motives. The government, through defense spending, public works, and otherwise, will unquestionably play a greater rôle in the future industrial development of the nation. Guiding principles in governmental industrial planning will of course differ in war and peace times. In war periods governmental industries are located primarily with regard to such factors as security of the plants from potential attack, proximity to needed supplies, materials, and labor, and delivery of finished products to the appropriate places of use or export. In peace times the dominating factors are likely to be the stabilization of employment, the development and conservation of our natural and human resources, and the promotion of a long-run, well-rounded, regional and national growth.

These governmental policies emphasize social considerations and long-run welfare. In some respects they conflict with private enterprise forces which necessarily emphasize economic and short-run factors. One of the most difficult tasks of the future is going to be the working out of an effective compromise and balance between governmental planning and private enterprise.

In the problem of attracting to a region new industries under private ownership, the industry management becomes largely a passive factor, looking over the various offers, inducements, and possible localities with a view to locating where the most advantages combine with the fewest disadvantages. The active factor is the various agencies trying to attract the new industry to the region and to the particular locality concerned. These agencies are public and private. Public agencies include the various levels of government—Federal, state, and local. Private include chambers of commerce, railroads, power companies, and other groups expecting to reap benefits from the new industries. Private agencies can offer few tangible inducements, their efforts being confined largely to such intangible forms as advertising, showing off possible locations, and presenting arguments why one particular locality or site is superior to rival ones. These "booster" methods are likely to be, at best, honest attempts to attract new industries which will effectively balance the community's present industries and thereby increase and stabilize employment, incomes, and community growth. At worst, they often become unethical if not dishonest portrayals of the "wonderful advantages of this community" as a site for any or all proposed industries.

Public agencies, through their taxing and other powers, are in a position to offer tangible inducements to new industries. Since the power and the prestige of government are involved, public agencies should act as wisely and judiciously as possible. Sound public policy in a democracy requires that the long-run welfare of all the people be placed uppermost. The easy way may be to yield to the pressure groups wanting tax concessions, free plant sites, and other favors to new industry. The long-run good of the greatest number, including older industries already being taxed, may require that no such discriminations be made. The easy way may be to award defense contracts to large firms in the highly industrialized regions, whereas long-run welfare may call for a wide distribution of such business among small and medium-sized plants in many less highly industrialized areas. What may minister to the welfare of a particular community may run counter to the welfare of the nation at large, as when an army training camp is located in a swamp or a large amount of taxpayers' money is spent on rivers and harbors that have no commerce. One problem is to see clearly where the long-run, greatest-good-of-the-greatest-number lies. Another is to induce the persons responsible for government decisions to follow the vision, once the vision is seen. All of these difficulties mean that governmental policies regarding industrial location are hard to work out rationally, encounter political difficulties in enactment and administration, and are often confused as between Federal policies on the one hand and state and local policies on the other.

To expedite a needed and sound industrialization of the Southeast the Federal government could and should:

1. Place more defense industries in the region, especially of the kind that may readily be adapted to peace-time uses.

2. Espouse the principle of equalized educational opportunity for all children in the nation. This involves Federal aid to southern education and specifically trade and technical training to raise the skills of native labor.

3. Revise the freight rate structure so as to remove or greatly reduce the transportation handicap suffered by the region.

4. By appropriate rate controls develop alternative and competing forms of transportation to railroads, especially waterways and motor transport.

5. Eliminate existing wage differentials between the Southeast and the North gradually, so as to allow adjustments to be made with a minimum of disturbance to industry.

6. Foster in every possible way the transition of regional agriculture from cotton to diversified farming, not only to promote sounder health and better rural incomes but also to provide a wider and more profitable variety of agricultural raw materials for industry.

7. Strengthen the Forest Service and other agencies working for the conservation and wise development of our timber resources in order to provide a stable supplementary income to farmers and also an assured future supply of wood for the expanding forest products industries.

8. Subsidize more liberally all types of research that

promise to promote sound agricultural and industrial progress in the region. The research program of the TVA and of other regional agencies and institutions proves what can be done when research is concentrated on regional problems.

9. Allocate to the Southeast a generous proportion of future housing funds, in order to remove rural and urban slums, elevate living standards, improve workers' health and efficiency, and create needed employment.

10. Recognize the strategic geographic location of the Southeast in relation to Latin America by developing in the region a reasonable proportion of the commercial, industrial, warehousing and other facilities growing out of the increased trade.

11. Help to obtain a better adjustment of the supply of labor to the demand by such measures as assistance to migration, improved public employment agencies, and better dissemination of job information.

The states and local communities can aid sound industrialization by:

1. Making careful studies of their particular natural resources with a view to attracting only those new industries that will have a sound economic base and therefore reasonable assurance of success in their new location.

2. An examination of their present industrial pattern to see clearly what they have now and what types of new industries are most needed to supplement and round out the pattern. Avoidance of certain industries may be as essential to a rounded development as the acquisition of new industries. In planning the future industrial pattern, heavy industry should be balanced by light industry; durable goods industries by nondurable; seasonal industry with a summer peak by seasonal industry with a winter peak, and so on.

3. In locating new public institutions such as educational, charitable, recreational, and health facilities, giving careful regard to communities and sub-areas needing the employment and stimulation of new public enterprises.

4. Increased appropriations for, and emphasis on, trade and technical training for youth and adults, that labor skills may be appreciably raised within the region.

5. Careful examination of their tax structures to see that they are neither too severe nor too lenient on industry. Too severe taxation tends to discourage the coming of new industries and the expansion of old ones. Too lenient taxation means either that insufficient revenues are being raised to carry on essential governmental services or that industry is being relieved of its fair share of the burden while other classes are bearing too much of the burden. Desirable new industries are not likely to be won by offering tax concessions.

6. Encouragement of experiments in the ruralization of industry, by which industries locate in rural areas, using the labor of farm people when they are not busy on the farm. Care must be shown in the selection of such industries, both to protect the owners against relying on too stable a labor supply and to protect the workers against exploitation in wages and hours.

7. The planning by cities now for their long-range development by visualizing their future growth and guiding the same by conscious effort. By proper zoning and other regulations, industrial location within broad metropolitan areas can be so guided and controlled as to eliminate slum and blighted sections, expedite traffic flow, prevent smoke and other nuisances, and contribute effectively to the health and beautification of the cities of tomorrow.

8. Planning streets and highways so as to make commuting easier and cheaper. The present trend toward living outside of congested areas promises much in health, sound child development, more efficient workers for industry, and a plot of ground to "fall back on" when industry slackens. States, counties, and cities should cooperate in the wise guidance of this movement.

9. Building up the underlying *social* factors in industry. The general level of health and intelligence of the local

population counts in attracting or repelling worth-while industries; hence good schools, well-administered public and private health facilities and other agencies building up health and intelligence should have emphasis and support. Dissemination of birth control information is needed. Ambition and initiative are valuable qualities needing cultivation. Negroes must be trained for and allowed to enter a wider range of occupations. State and local government must be purged of incompetent and parasitic office holders so that the taxpayers' dollars, which mean real sacrifices for most taxpayers in low income regions, shall obtain effective and economical governmental services. A gradual elevation of the whole plane of southeastern life will offer good industries a more inviting environment. In last analysis the Southeast must take the chief responsibility for its own improvement. It must pull itself up. It must pull *all* of itself up.

# Twentieth Century South-wide Civic & Lay Organizations for Human Welfare

*LYDA GORDON SHIVERS*
*Associate Professor of Sociology*

A SALIENT characteristic of the regional picture of social welfare in the South is the importance of the socially minded layman. The fact that the technical and professional development of social work in the region before 1917 was confined largely to a few urban communities indicates that, outside of these centers, the reflective, intelligent layman was the dominant figure in the broader, regional social programs initiated in the earlier decades of the twentieth century. The rosters of the pioneer conferences list the names of laymen who were to become future technicians in social work as well as future civic leaders in state conferences of social service and in the various citizens' fact-finding movements of Georgia, North Carolina, and other southern states. A study of the programs, leaders, and emphases of these conferences is a method of revealing the major concerns of the day, as perceived by thinking people, and of indicating changing social philosophies and concepts of responsibility.

An exhaustive list of all the region-wide agencies having as their goal some amelioration of social conditions in the Southeast would total an impressive figure: abundant evidence of either the Southerner's faith or his sociability. Organizations have differed widely in their prestige, duration, objectives, and achievements. It may be assumed that some societies have been so ephemeral that no record of their existence remains. The following general organizations are listed in chronological order and presented as a tentative enumeration of the significant South-wide groups in the period 1900-1940:

Conference for Education in the South (1898-1914)

Conference of the Society for the Consideration of the Race Problems and Conditions of the South (?1900 meeting only record)

Southern Sociological Congress (1912-1920)

University Commission on Race Questions (1912-1925)

Conference of Southern Mountain Workers (1913-)

Southern Woman's Educational Alliance (1914-1937. Name and functions changed: now Alliance for Guidance of Rural Youth, a national agency centering on rural guidance)

The Southern Conference for Education and Industry (1915-1916)

Southern Publicity Committee (1918-1921)

Commission on Interracial Cooperation (1919-)

Southern Governors' Conference (? Met at least as early as 1911; very informal until the 1930's)

Blue Ridge Institute for Social Work Executives (1927-)

Southeastern Council (1929-)

Association of Southern Women for the Prevention of Lynching (1930-)

Southern Council for Women and Children in Industry (1931-?)

Southern State Industrial Council (1933-)

Southeastern Interstate Conference on Social Legislation (1933-. Meets on call of Secretary of Labor)

Southern Policy Association (1935-1937)

Southern Conference for Human Welfare (1938-)

Council of Young Southerners (1939-)

Southern Conference on Tomorrow's Children (1939-)

Additional region-wide organizations may be classified either as regional associations of national groups or as special regional societies based upon community interest. Examples of the first are: Southern Regional Child Welfare Conference, Southern Regional Conference American Association of Social Workers, and Southern Conference of Progressive Education Association. Illustrations of special regional societies are: Southern Society for Philosophy and Psychology, Southeastern Library Association, Southern Historical Association, and Southern Sociological Society. These groupings are indicated for perspective.

The subject matter under consideration relates to the general conference type, organized and supported principally by southern laymen, and with catholic objectives for human welfare. Conference for Education in the South, Southern Conference for Education and Industry, Southern Sociological Congress, Southern Policy Association, and Southern Conference for Human Welfare are five conferences which exemplify these traits.[1] There is a time spread of forty years from the first meeting of the pioneer conference to the first meeting of the newest of these regional civic movements. Do any important differences emerge?

An understanding of the cultural background of the region is necessary to distinguish nuances in the tone of the conference speeches. The early southern sociologists were not only stating theoretical concepts to support the economic and social life of the ante-bellum period, but their brilliant deductions were still a part of much southern philosophy at the beginning of the century. An integral part of the pattern was the concept of the responsibilities of a superior people for an inferior. *Noblesse oblige* was a motivating force in causing southern liberals to work for the social welfare of the Negro and also of the poor white. Whatever oratorical tributes are paid to democracy in the pioneer programs, a careful reading of the proceedings provides abundant proof that the vitalizing force is a strong sense of responsibility. This has been well stated by Mr. Edgar Gardner Murphy, an outstanding leader in the early conference movement: "The sense of responsibility may express itself wisely or mistakenly, preversely or constructively, but whatever the form of its expression, the consciousness of obligation is not absent."

In the conferences organized after 1930 the trend is toward stress upon democratic processes. The right of every citizen to participate in the process, as well as the duty of active participation, is emphasized. It is indicated that a citizens' movement must be essentially democratic. The conferences took positive stands for poll tax reform. At its first meeting the Southern Conference for Human Welfare (1938-) resolved to go on record for: enactment of Federal and state legislation to establish uniform registration laws; elimination of the poll tax; and liberalization of election laws with respect to the requirements for printing names of parties and independent candidates on the ballot. The Council of Young Southerners, established in 1939, has as its purpose the awakening of young people in the South to a greater interest in public affairs and a more active participation in government.

Other indices of change in the lay conferences are indicated by a comparison of membership, participation of Negroes, section meetings, and southern criticism. A diverse membership has always been a marked feature of these groups. Conferences have had memberships drawn from many occupations: teaching, law, politics, business, ministry, medicine, industry, agriculture, and others. However, in the Southern Conference for Human Welfare two new groups are represented: the tenant farmer and labor organizations. When the National Conference of Charities and Correction met in the South in 1903, a commentator mentioned the fact that no Negroes were present at the meetings. Another northern commentator writing about the Conference for Education in the South, meeting in Columbia, South Carolina, in 1905, is critical because Negroes were seated only in the balcony. He apparently was not aware that it was unusual for them to be present in any status. Negroes were accepted as delegates to the Southern Sociological Congress. There were occasional Negro speakers, and Negroes took part in informal discussion in the section meetings. At the conference meeting in 1913 there was a spirit of optimism concerning future race relations. It was said that this meeting was of historic significance since it marked the first time in the South that Negroes and whites met on a basis of intellectual equality to discuss their common problems. It is a minor irony, in view of recent occurrences in Georgia, that this was in Atlanta in 1913. In its plan of organization the Southern Conference for Human Welfare (1938-) provided: "the governing body shall be a Southern Council representative of the entire region, of all fields of endeavor, and of all social and racial groups. . . ."

Three of the conferences have had sectional meetings. A study of the names of the different sections is one method of presenting the range of the conference programs. The Conference for Education in the South (1898-1914) did not use the term sectional meetings, but "conferences meeting in conjunction with it." Actually they constituted sectional meetings rather than autonomous conferences. They were fundamentally occupational groups, the basic idea being that each had special approaches and problems relating to education and general human welfare. By 1913 these alignments were: The Farmers' Conference, Country Church Conference, Business Men's Conference, Southern Association of College Women, and Conference of Country Doctors. The Southern Sociological Congress (1912-1920) adopted the usual plan of sectional divisions. At its first meeting the Congress was sectioned into the following subdivisions: child welfare, courts and prisons, public health, Negro problems, education and coöperation, church and social service, and the call and qualifications of social workers. At its second convention there were still seven sections. Identical terminology was used for four; but "Negro problems" was broadened to "race problems," "organized charity" replaced "call and qualifications of social workers," travelers' aid was added, and the section on education and coöperation was dropped. Meeting twenty-five years later the Southern Conference for Human Welfare (1938-) gave time on its program to three sections for two sessions, the second meeting being restricted to delegates. These emphasized sections were on farm tenancy, constitutional rights, and labor relations and unemployment. Other divisional assemblies took up the following topics: credit, education, prison reform, housing, suffrage, race relations, women wage earners, freight rate differentials, youth problems, health, and child labor.

It is dangerous to generalize concerning the extent to which these various civic movements have represented general regional attitudes. Nevertheless, conferences of laymen are an important part of the southern regional picture in the realm of social welfare. These organizations have played their rôles in terms of impelling and stimulating public interest and action in social welfare in the South. In terms of future social planning, the record of their failures is as important as is that of their successes. For purposes of social planning, if for no other cause, the life pattern of these organizations merits analysis, and their history merits writing.

The leaders of the civic movement initiated by southern educators in the first decade of the twentieth century were individuals deeply concerned with the welfare of persons. They sincerely believed in education as the South's catholicon. The Conference for Education in the South is the first of the major civic movements. It was founded in 1898 and for two years was known as the Conference on Christian Education in the South. Its purpose was to elevate the "ignorant and destitute, black and white," of the South. This was to be accomplished through the promotion of democratic education "as the surest and only means to the solution of all our problems of industrial, economic, social, civic and political life." At the first meeting at Capon

Springs, West Virginia, members were invited to be present and twenty-seven came. After the original meeting the only qualification for delegates were "personal appearance" and "sympathetic accord." This conference never was a professional organization. It was a propaganda agency for the promotion of human welfare, the means to the accomplishment of which was the promotion of education. "In an effort of genuine civic consecration, men of affairs from every department of activity—merchants, members of Congress, journalists, governors of states, bankers, and manufacturers have united with the educators of the South in an effort to equip and extend the school as an institution of society itself."

By 1909 a more accurate designation would have been a country life conference. Typical speeches dealt with such topics as greater production, better use of the soil, better homes, better health conditions, better rural conditions, and better educational facilities. This trend continued in the remainder of the conference meetings. When the conference met in Richmond in 1913, over twenty-three hundred men and women were present. It was still a group drawn from various occupations: farmers, businessmen, college presidents, schoolteachers, representatives of local credit associations, and ministers. Walter Hines Page was present and added prestige as the coming Ambassador to the Court of St. James. The theme of the conference was rural education and emphasis was placed upon the opportunities for life presented in rural regions. The conference has always been an idealistic body, but in this particular conference the reporter reiterates the religious spirit of the gathering. The conference covered far more than simply rural education; it included the relationship of agricultural coöperation and better farm credits to other topics discussed: school, church, home, and business. This wide inclusion was justified because "the South's machinery for social amelioration was largely educational."

The Conference for Education in the South consolidated

with the Southern Educational Association and the Southern Education Board in 1914 to form the Southern Conference for Education and Industry.

The Conference for Education in the South published annual reports. These provide the source material for a summary of its record. During its seventeen years of existence, the conference had only four presidents: the Reverend T. V. Dudly, Dr. J. L. M. Curry, Mr. Robert C. Ogden of New York, and Mr. F. R. Chambers. Mr. Ogden served as president of the conference for fourteen years, and gave generous financial support. It was through his courtesy that a number of northern members were brought down by special train each year. Mr. Ogden played such a prominent rôle that opponents of the activities of the conference dubbed them "Ogdenites." There were probably two reasons for opposition. One was the insistence of the conference upon adequate education for the Negro people, a radical stand at the particular time; the second was the feeling that this was another effort under northern leadership to patronize the South. The two publications which led the attack were the *Charleston News and Courier* and the *Manufacturer's Record*. However, the opposition never was very serious, and in 1909 the Atlanta Chamber of Commerce gave a reception and presented Mr. Ogden with a loving cup in recognition of his services. The average Southerner seems to have welcomed philanthropy; the wail of a distinguished southern bishop was the plaint of a small minority:

There are certain groups of Southerners who have injured the South in the North and in Europe by a mischievous mendicancy. These are they who have been ready to run to Northern millionaires for money to endow our colleges and even for money to cure the alleged diseases of some of our people. Thereby they have advertized the South as a section teeming with ignorance, stinginess, mortal diseases and degenerates who were made degenerates by their ailments. . . . Our people are able and willing to solve their own education promlems. We do not need to beg any man to pay our school bills or to teach us how to conduct our educational institutions. . . . Much ado has been made about the hookworm in the South and Rockefeller has seen fit to give a large sum to be used in purging Southern people of alleged lazy bugs. It is enough to say that any and all of our people are quite able to pay their own doctors' bills. We are able to treat our own patients and we would be still more able to care for them if our section were not so constantly advertized to its hurt by our mendicant theorists and reformers. What the South needs very much is to be let alone.[2]

The leaders of this pioneer conference were tactful and fully aware of the mores of the region. It was a conference for action. The technique was to work within the regional mores rather than to arouse antagonism by shock tactics. The following quotation is a brilliant example of the presentation of what was a radical idea in accepted phraseology. It is taken from an address to an audience of the Conference for the Consideration of the Race Problems and Conditions of the South, delivered at Montgomery, Alabama, on May 9, 1900, by a distinguished southern educator and leader—former president of the education conference.

The negro is a valuable laborer; let us improve him and make his labor more intelligent, more skilled, more productive. . . . Shall the Caucasian race, in timid fearfulness, in cowardly injustice, wrong an inferior race, put obstacles to its progress? Left to itself, away from the elevating influence of contact and tuition, there will be retrogression. Shall we hasten the retrogression, shall we have two races side by side, equal in political privileges, one educated, the other ignorant? Unless the white people, the superior, the cultivated race, lift up the lower, both will be inevitably dragged down.

Look at these roses on this platform. They have been developed from an inferior plant by skilled culture into gorgeous American Beauties. So it is with other flowers and fruits; so with animals, and so it is with men. Eight hundred years ago our ancestors were pirates, careless of laws, either of God or man, and yet by culture and education, and discipline and free institutions and liberty of worship, they have been made the people that they are today. God's throne is justice and right and truth. Unseat Him from that throne and He becomes a demon; and so will sink our Southern civilization into infamy if we are guilty of cruelest injustice to an inferior race. whom God has put into our hands as trustees for their elevation and improvement, and for His glory.[3]

Mr. Edgar Gardner Murphy has reported with what deep emotion and sincere approval this peroration was received by the audience. The word "inferiority" is used, but the fact that it is economic inferiority which is stressed, rather than biological, probably escaped the audience.

Growing out of the need for more aggressive action than could be attempted through an annual conference, the Southern Education Board was organized in 1901. The membership of this original board is interesting: it included in addition to Mr. Ogden, the agent of the Peabody and Slater Boards, Mr. George Foster Peabody, Mr. Charles D. McIver of North Carolina, Dr. Charles W. Dabney, President of the University of Cincinnati, Dr. Edwin A. Alderman, then President of Tulane, Dr. Wallace Buttrick, secretary of the General Education Board, and Dr. H. B. Frissell, principal of Hampton Institute. Mr. Edgar Gardner Murphy of Alabama became the board's secretary. The conferences were not abandoned after the creation of the board, but continued to act as a force in awakening popular interest and as an interpreter of the policies of the board. The active work of the board was put in the hands of a "Campaign Committee" composed of the southern members. It was frankly a work of propaganda to arouse and wisely to direct educational sentiment in the South. It emphasized especially the work of the public school, in some cases inaugurating and in others lending support to local movements for increased taxation for school purposes.

The conference had all its annual meetings, after the first two, in the Southeast. Louisiana and Mississippi were the only states without a conference meeting. In chronological order the meetings were held in the following communities: Capon Springs, West Virginia; Winston-Salem, North Carolina; Athens, Georgia; Richmond, Virginia; Birmingham, Alabama; Columbia, South Carolina; Lexington, Kentucky; Pinehurst, North Carolina; Memphis, Tennessee; Atlanta, Georgia; Little Rock, Arkansas; Jacksonville, Florida;

Nashville, Tennessee; Richmond, Virginia; Louisville, Kentucky.

At the final meeting of the Conference for Education in the South, Mr. P. P. Claxton delivered an address summarizing its achievements and history. Other agencies and movements had grown out of the conference and the work of the Southern Education Board. Mr. Claxton stated these to be the General Education Board, the Farmers' Coöperative Demonstration Work (Knapp Movement), and the Rockefeller Sanitary Commission for the Eradication of the Hookworm Disease. The conference was an effective agency for human welfare during the first ten years of the century. It was well adjusted to meet obvious needs of that period. It proved incapable, however, of accommodating to changing circumstances and new emphases. The emotional impetus, so important a contribution in propagandism, is the chief explanation of its loss of prestige in the second decade.

Southern leaders by 1910 were writing that the South should free itself of emphasis on a single issue. Absorption in one major problem was disastrous, and too much attention had been given to the Negro question. There was too little discussion of other large vital questions. The general tone was to the effect that the South had been too much on the defensive, had spent too large a portion of its energy on matters of small importance. It was fitting that it should revaluate its human needs and furnish its own constructive criticism.

Miss Kate Barnard, Commissioner of Charities and Corrections in Oklahoma, wrote in December, 1911, to Governor Ben W. Hooper of Tennessee suggesting that he call a southern conference to study and discuss southern problems. Governor Hooper had shown great interest in social welfare during his governorship of Tennessee. He sent out a letter to the other governors of the southern states asking them to appoint not less than one hundred delegates to meet in Nashville in May, 1912. Over seven hundred people attended this meeting, and the Southern Sociological Congress was organized. It was put on a sound financial basis by a private gift, and it was agreed to make the congress an annual meeting. The policy of the congress at its first two meetings was strictly pragmatic. Discussion was practical, based upon important social problems in the South and the possibilities of remedying them. The general attitude was that the need was not theory but action. In spite of the use of the term sociological in its title, the congress was not concerned with sociology in theory. The concept of sociology was not that of the modern university subject but that of a practical tool for social reform. The purpose of the congress was the study and improvement of the social and economic conditions of the South. In its later history it dealt more with the development of social conscience. The slogan of the conference was: "The Solid South for a Better Nation."

The second annual meeting lasted four days and over eight hundred delegates attended. There were ninety-six speakers. The most important and largest sectional meeting, judged by the attendance and number of speakers, was the section on race problems. It is stated that some of the Negro delegates, expecting discrimination against them in the conference sections, had prepared while on the way to Atlanta resolutions of protest. These were never presented, no occasion arising for their use. In 1914, the National Conference of Charities and Correction met in Memphis and the Southern Sociological Congress met in conjunction with it. By special agreement, the congress confined its part on the program to race relations and the church and social service. The other departments were in charge of the national conference. This led to a certain amount of open criticism on the part of the congress membership, some members feeling that the conference was too religious, and other groups objecting to the amount of time devoted to race problems. At this time the congress had a membership of approximately seventeen hundred, of whom about two hundred and fifty were people residing outside the southern region.

Houston, Texas, was the site of the 1915 meeting, and the theme was the conservation of health. The congress embarked upon a definite program of health education to be carried out under the direction of six commissions. The procedure and policies of this meeting mark the beginning of the steady decline of the congress's influence as a regional agency. There was a great chasm between the original purpose, which was an objective, realistic analysis of regional needs and intelligent programs of action, and the actuality of the Houston meeting. The tenor of the program was toward an emotional revivalism. The "Congress Battle Hymn" to the tune of "Tipperary" is all too typical of the general atmosphere:

IT'S A HARD FIGHT TO SAVE THE CHILDREN

Through our sunny Southern land there spreads encircling gloom,
Leaving anxious sorrow in the heart of every home,
For the silent fiend Disease is stalking o'er the land
To smite the little children with his deadly poison hand.

*Chorus*

It's a hard fight to save the children;
It's a hard fight we know.
It's a hard fight to save the children,
But the fiend Disease must go.
Come, men, for hearth and homeland,
Play up, do your share!
It's a hard, hard fight to save the children;
But Old South's right there.

Hail ye, doctor captains, on your farflung fever line;
And ye preacher pickets, brave with love of life divine;
Rouse, ye sons of Lee and Lincoln, heed the will of God,
Who never meant a darling child to sleep beneath the sod.
Should this smiling playground of the nation's children dear
Frown with tiny orphaned graves that make the mothers fear?
Hark, O men! a million children's bitter wail of woe;
*For this, God's chorus call: "The Fiend Disease must go!"*

In 1916 the Southern Sociological Congress met in New Orleans, where the Southern Conference for Education and Industry was meeting. This latter conference, successor to the Conference for Education in the South, was organized in 1915, held two meetings, and left no further record. It was completely dominated by an emotional religious approach encouraged by fervid eloquence on the part of its speakers. The movement was captured in its early stages by the dominant personality of a leading minister. The general atmosphere is indicated by the newspaper reports: "The South knows its troubles and is not ashamed to pray over them." "The cordial, sincere religious life of the South has a better chance to contribute a Christian spirit to the economic struggle than in any other part of the country. Diversified farming is being made a matter of morality and religion. There was something difficult to express in this great conference. The meetings were all held in a certain atmosphere, the handshaking in the halls, the casual contacts between workers of different sorts, voice something that one strives in vain to express."

The coöperation with this conference encouraged the Southern Sociological Congress to continue in the same pattern. The congress continued to plan a health campaign. Ten cities were chosen in which social surveys would be made and health campaigns fostered. Plans were made for extension conferences, and an extension secretary was appointed.

The congress steadily lost in importance and influence. Headquarters were moved from Nashville to Washington, and an effort was made to have it become a national organization. The effect of the war was to focus the attention of the congress at its Blue Ridge meeting primarily on wartime social problems. By 1918 the Southern Sociological Congress, while it had presented a few factual papers at the Birmingham conference, conceived of itself fundamentally as an inspirational organization. It continued to lose in prestige and influence. A meeting was held in 1919 and a final one in 1920, but the attendance was very small and largely limited to ministers or former ministers engaged in social work. In 1919 the southern territory was divided.

With the exception of the years 1916 and 1917 the Southern Sociological Congress published its proceedings. J. E. McCulloch served as editor. The titles of these volumes are significant and in themselves indicative of motivation. The following is a statement of titles with the date of publication: *The Call of the New South*, 1912; *The South Mobilizing for Social Service*, 1913; *Battling for Social Betterment*, 1914; *The New Chivalry—Health*, 1915; *Democracy in Earnest*, 1918; and *Distinguished Service Citizenship*, 1919. Among the presidents of the congress were three governors: Ben W. Hooper of Tennessee, William Hodges Mann of Virginia, and Charles H. Brough of Arkansas. Among other presidents were the Reverend A. J. McKelway of Washington, Bishop Theodore D. Bratton of Mississippi, and Dr. Samuel P. Brooks of Texas.

It is easy to exaggerate the impuissance of the Southern Sociological Congress. Its unfulfilled potentialities for the social welfare of the region were so significant that its real achievements appear futile. It was the paramount regional organization for human welfare in the second decade of the century. Observing its procedures in the midst of the regional opportunities, the critic is tempted to write *vox et praeterea nihil*. Yet it left an imprint upon the region particularly as a consequence of its first two meetings. It seems to have been a pioneer in having leading members of both races meet to discuss common problems. The University Commission on the Race Question was organized as an outgrowth of the first meeting of the congress. The development of state conferences for social service was influenced by the regional agency. The strong North Carolina conference was organized by state leaders as a direct result. Other state conferences were stimulated by the congress meetings. The intangible results are difficult to measure, but undoubtedly some laymen were more active in the state programs of social welfare as a result of attending the congress. The major cause of its final loss of prestige appears to have been too great mobilization of emotion without sufficient information or adequate leadership.

There was no other important south-wide laymen's organization with the broad objective of promoting general human welfare until the organization of the Southern Policy Association in 1935. A year before, small groups had been formed in several southern states with the design of studying regional and national policies on a firm factual basis, especially those with local implications. The groups were in touch with each other; there was some exchange of views. The Foreign Policy Association sponsored a meeting of these groups in Atlanta in 1935. Mr. Francis Pickens Miller was active in arousing interest in the meeting, and Mr. H. C. Nixon was the first president. About thirty people attended this meeting. A second conference was held in Chattanooga in 1936 on the general subject of "Social Security for the South—Urban and Rural." Specific topics considered were: agricultural social security, industrial social security, the constitution and social security, and democratic institutions. In 1937 the Southern Policy Association was absorbed by the National Policy Committee, and since then Southern Regional Conferences of the National Policy Committee have been held in 1938 in Atlanta, and in 1940 in Southern Pines.

The Southern Policy Association attracted a small but notable group of southern intellectuals, mostly college professors, authors, newspaper editors, and social philosophers. The association functioned through the Southern Policy Committee, which encouraged the development of state and local committees. It was hoped that the local groups would serve as centers of political discussion and thus prepare themselves for intelligent political action. An important contribution of the regional committee would be to place at the disposal of the local committees relevant factual material from competent research. Two of the most effective state policy committees were in Alabama and Arkansas. The Arkansas Committee—with a membership of over one hundred—published in 1936 an excellent pamphlet on *Agricultural Labor Problems in Arkansas.*

The *Southern Policy Papers* were issued by the regional committee through the University of North Carolina Press. The purpose of these pamphlets was to stimulate interest in questions of public importance in the region. The range of these papers is indicated by the following three, first published: T. J. Woofter, Jr., *Southern Population and Social Planning;* H. Clarence Nixon, *Social Security for Southern Farmers;* and Charles W. Pipkin, *Social Legislation in the South.*

The question of whether the Southern Policy Association should remain, as its name implied, an organization interested primarily in policies, or whether it should serve as an action and pressure group, was a source of much discussion. The subsidiary organizations in the states were frequently active as well as research groups. A large portion of the membership was definitely interested in initiating and supporting programs for human welfare. It was felt, however, that perhaps a more effective procedure would be to establish a new organization for programs of action. This proposal was discussed at a meeting of the Southern Policy Committee in 1937 and again in the spring of 1938. Individual members believed that Southerners, effectively organized, could make progress in remedying the ills of the region. The committee reached the decision that the work of coördinating the efforts of liberal and progressive groups in the South to formulate some program for action should be undertaken by another organization, which could utilize the research of the committee and of other groups.

The reaction to the National Emergency Council's *Report on Economic Conditions of the South* and the discussions of the Southern Policy Committee resulted in the organization of a new conference. The Southern Conference for Human Welfare held its first meeting in Birmingham in the fall of 1938. Seventy-nine Southerners representing all the states of the region served as sponsors. Judge Louise O. Charlton served as general chairman, and Dr. H. C. Nixon was field chairman. Dr. Nixon later became the executive secretary of the conference. There was an attendance of approximately twelve hundred. No one could be a delegate to this conference unless a Southerner by birth or residence. Visitors were invited, but decisions of the conference were to be decisions arrived at by Southerners. On the program were national leaders with much prestige, as well as prominent regional representatives. The purposes of the conference were: to coördinate the efforts of many liberal and progressive groups throughout the South; to formulate plans for the correction of southern deficiencies; and to establish an organization to continue work in the future. The conference adopted a long and elaborate list of resolutions relating to a wide range of subject matter.

The first meeting of the conference received national and regional publicity. The second meeting, held under the chairmanship of President Frank Graham in Chattanooga, received much less notice outside the region. The theme of this meeting was "Democracy in the South."

It is impossible at the present time to evaluate this organization in the general regional conference picture. Criticism of the conference arose within the South as a result of the first meeting. Certain local mores were disregarded by some members of the conference. A typical criticism was that the conference was under too radical influence and had Communist support. Whether this conference has the leadership and the program to mobilize effectively the intelligent, interested Southerner in the promotion of human welfare is a question for the future. Certainly it has available more information than any previous regional conference has had.

There have been, as already indicated, other regional agencies with more specific objectives and operating within a narrower range of interest. As illustrative of this type of lay organization, a brief résumé is given of the agencies for the promotion of interracial relationships. These groups represent important regional emphases.

The University Commission on the Race Question was organized in 1912 by Dr. James A. Dillard. The purpose of this organization was for the universities to take a position of leadership and provide "stimulation for the lot of the Negro to enable him to gain better opportunities among all lines of endeavor." Members of the commission were appointed officially by the faculties of their respective universities. The advisory committee of the Commission in 1914 consisted of Dr. Dillard, Dr. Alderman of the University of Virginia, Chancellor Barrow of the University of Georgia, and President Mitchell of the Medical College of Virginia. There were annual meetings, often held in conjunction with the Southern Sociological Congress. Periodical letters were issued, directed especially to the college students of the South. The letter against lynching issued in 1916 received the greatest publicity of the commission's history. In the letter issued at the meeting in Knoxville in 1922 all the evidences of interracial coöperation were pointed out. A previous letter called attention to the fact that college men were expected to assist in molding public opinion and to coöperate in all similar efforts to bring about a more tolerant spirit and a larger measure of good will and understanding between the best elements of both races. These are typical emphases. The commission became inactive in 1925.

The Southern Publicity Committee was in existence between 1917 and 1921. Its primary purpose was to advertise in the South some of the South's constructive work in racial matters. The Commission on Interracial Coöperation was established in 1919. This has been the most important regional organization for the specific purpose of promoting interracial good will. Its purpose is "to correct interracial neglect and injustice, to better conditions affecting Negroes, and to improve those interracial attitudes out of which unfavorable conditions grow." The commission is composed of over one hundred men and women, white and Negro, in positions of leadership in the South. Affiliated with it are several state and local committees similarly constituted. The groups are autonomous but maintain close relationship with the commission. The headquarters of the commission is in Atlanta. Will W. Alexander, R. B. Eleazer, and Mrs. Jesse Daniel Ames have been active executives in this organization. Among its presidents have been such outstanding Southerners as Ashby Jones, Walter C. Jackson, John Hope, McNeill Poteat, and Howard W. Odum. The Association of Southern Women for the Prevention of Lynching was organized in 1930, sponsored by the Commission on Interracial Coöperation. Its name indicates its purpose.

What should characterize future regional developments? A regional conference has value as a clearing house for ideas of human welfare, regardless of the value of any schemes for social well-being which it may germinate. Many intelligent Southerners have an interest in the Southeast and in its human needs. This interest, informed and realistic, is a regional resource of value. Regional social planning should consider the potentialities of such a group. Social progress advances securely only as it carries with it an educated and enlightened public opinion. An important function of an adequate regional organization is to inform lay leaders of advances in social knowledge and to enlist their advice and aid in constructive planning.

Immediate needs are for a clarification of goals and techniques and a correlation of the activities of various existing groups. Familiar terminology in the Southeast is the "Committee of One Hundred." One hundred leading southern laymen might be designated as a group to work out the best procedures for utilizing the resources of lay social interest. Existing organizations would send representatives to coöperate with this group. The organization representations would present the objectives, techniques, and programs of their respective bodies. There is value, however, in having the planning group distinct from existing regional agencies. The various state conferences of social service in the Southeast, with the exceptions of two states, have had an important lay membership. Until very recent years, they have been predominantly state lay organizations for human welfare. It might be feasible that these conferences sponsor a regional planning committee.

Past history indicates that careful study and planning should precede any organizing procedures. Previous conferences have been successful in mobilizing emotion for action, but their leaders and programs have too frequently been inadequate. A regional program for human welfare should have as an objective the use of the region's human resources in interest and intelligence. What form and type of regional organization is most effective for this purpose should be determined only after a group of the region's leaders have given careful study to the proposals and conclusions of students of regional social planning.

[illegible] effectiveness.[illegible] There is nothing, however, in having the planning group distinct from existing regional agencies, the [illegible] experiences of social research in the Southeast [illegible] the governors of [illegible] states have [illegible] by the universities [illegible] years [illegible] have been [illegible] written. In [illegible] these [illegible] a regional planning [illegible]

But [illegible] that careful study and planning should precede [illegible] centers [illegible] have been [illegible] action, [illegible] programs have [illegible] been [illegible]. A regional program [illegible] would [illegible] the use of the regions [illegible]. We [illegible] would be [illegible] of the regional [illegible] we [illegible] the [illegible] of [illegible] social planning.

# Earth & Man:

# The European Heritage

*EDNA ARUNDEL*
*Assistant Professor of Geography*

SINCE THE DAYS of ancient Greece and Rome, social philosophers have pondered over the relationship of man to his environment. For many centuries, they have made observations and accumulated facts, which in turn have been claimed by the various social sciences. As the history of these sciences has evolved, certain trends have revealed themselves, and definite points of emphases have been detected. A heritage, descending from the time of Hippocrates, Bodin, and Montesquieu, exists. What are the trends and emphases of the European heritage that have influenced American geographic-social thought?

The social philosophers of ancient Greece and Rome were concerned about such questions as the superiority of Greek over Barbarian, or the preëminence in military acumen of soldiers from the intermediate climes over those who were unfortunate enough to have spent their lives in the hotter and colder regions of the globe. To these early philosophers, the environment seemed all-powerful. They believed themselves to be in a state of subjection to unwritten laws of rigid, fatalistic determinism. Hippocrates (460-370 B.C.), interested in the relationship of man and environment from a medical point of view, developed some rather close correlations between diseases of man and the different seasons and climates. From his various observations, he brought forth some interesting generalizations concerning peoples of his time. He noted that the climate of Asia produced people with gentle, affectionate dispositions, who were intelligent and inventive. However, this type of physical environment lulled its population into a state of feebleness of spirit, and as a consequence these peoples were content to remain in a state of slavery and subjection to their masters. In contrast, he observed that the Europeans had variety, vigor, and fierceness, and that they were more progressive. He believed that a climate is needed which would "give excitement to the understanding," would ruffle the emotions, and would force people to a state of bravery and exertion.[1] His conclusions are interesting, especially when they are considered in the light of their ancient setting, and in view of our present developments.

Of the early modern social philosophers, the first writer to attempt a systematic discussion of the influences of physical environment upon man was Jean Bodin (1530-1596), a French political philosopher. *The Fifthe Booke of a Commonweale*[2] contains his environmental theories, in which he attempted to formulate a general law for the guidance of statesmen in manipulating "the diversities of men's humours." He predicted failure in the careers of statesmen and nations that ignored this factor in the formulation and enforcement of laws; he agreed with the ancient philosophers that climate affects the "humours" of men; he discussed at length the differences between northern, southern, and middle-latitude Europeans. Of these groups, men of the middle-latitude areas had the better climatic conditions, and thus were "better tempered in wit and bodie," and were "of sanguine and choleric humor, like people of middle age." According to Bodin's observations, men of temperate zone areas, truthful and reliable, were adapted to govern the peoples of the more inferior climatic realms. Topography, climate, and location were the three geographical factors which he considered the most influential in the development of men and nations. He attributed France's rank as the foremost nation of the world to her superior location in respect to important bodies of water and in relation to European countries. Although Bodin's theories were a summation of all that had gone before him, and were impregnated with physical philosophy and astrology, he nevertheless made a contribution to social theory. He attempted an analysis and a systematic arrangement of all existing theories; and, more valuable, he directly applied these theories to the field of statesmanship, where they would be used and developed by others.

Up to the time of Karl Ritter, the most extensive treatment of man and environment was that of Montesquieu, the French publicist, one of the greatest social theorists of the eighteenth century. He believed that men in political life should frame the laws in relation to the nature of the climate, the quality of the soil, the kinds of products and commercial relations, the number of persons being governed, the manner of living of the inhabitants, and the inclinations of the people—their religion, their natural wealth, their manners and customs. He felt that the laws should fit each regional group, and that the culture which had been evolving in each region for centuries, should be recognized. Like Bodin and the early philosophers, he believed that climate had been the chief determinant of physical characteristics, and, therefore, of political qualities. His contribution to the thinking of his time lies in the use of an inductive, comparative method of ascertaining the results of geographical influences upon society. As *The Spirit of Laws*[3] implies, ". . . 'tis not so much my business to follow the natural order of laws, as that of these relations and things." He was interested in environmental influences primarily from the point of view of the lawmaker, and he was concerned chiefly about "the spirit" that underlies written laws.

The first social philosopher to investigate the relationship between physical environment and the mind of man was

Henry Thomas Buckle (1821-1862), who expressed his ideas in the *History of Civilization in England*.[4] He was interested in the influences of environment not only upon the individual mind and character, but also upon the nation as a whole. His analysis centered around four factors of the geographical environment: climate, soil, food, and the general aspect of nature. He described climate, soil, and food as being dependent upon each other; and since they had an indirect effect upon the minds of men, he designated them also as determinants of man's behavior. He believed that climate was responsible for man's energy, that soil was the basis of wealth and culture, and that the wages of the workers, the food supply, and high or low birth rates were intimately connected. These three factors were interrelated in many different ways in his analysis. But, as a determiner of man's mind, the fourth factor was given the greatest weight.

Buckle saw a definite connection between the general aspect of nature and mental qualities. His illustrations were taken not only from present history, but also from the remote periods of civilization. He pointed to the early peoples that had developed in the warm, tropical areas. Here, nature with its earthquakes, hurricanes, its exuberance of plants and animals, was exciting and even dangerous. He observed that threatening conditions stimulated the mind, particularly its imaginative qualities, aroused superstition, but discouraged knowledge of a scientific nature. He contrasted India and Greece as the examples of two types of mental development. The tropical conditions of India—its high mountains, great plains, hot climates, heavy rainfalls—have there produced a type of character that loves the superhuman and unnatural. These conditions brought forth the imaginative qualities that are represented in her literature, philosophy, and ceremonial life. In India, man became intimidated, depressed, and inspired by fear of an all-powerful nature. The opposite condition evolved in Greece, where nature was more composed and the process of reasoning more developed. There everything tended toward a respect for the dignity of man. That tendency gave the Greek confidence in his development, and a respect for human power and ability. Buckle noted the achievements of the north temperate zone in scientific accomplishments and attributed these to a healthier climate, fewer earthquakes, less disastrous hurricanes, and fewer dangerous animals. Man, in such an environment, could order his reasoning powers; and as a result, science could develop. Though Buckle's work may have lacked system and was subject to generalizations without adequate proof, yet he offered an original analysis. This analysis is important, particularly in the light of more recent developments, such as the measurement of human efficiency in relation to climatic regions, which has been developed by Ellsworth Huntington in *Civilization and Climate*.[5] Buckle definitely placed nature as the determinant of the mind and character of man: "Everywhere the hand of Nature is upon us, and . . . the history of the human mind can only be understood by connecting with it the history and the aspects of the material universe."

Although the relations of man and environment provoked thinking and writing in the early and modern periods of history, little progress had been made in extensive, scientific studies from actual regions of the earth. Much of the thinking was merely "a belief" of certain men, such as the Arab geographers who believed that all great philosophers and religious leaders were born within a certain number of degrees of latitude, to be exact—between twenty-nine and thirty-three degrees, forty-nine minutes north latitude. They had facts; but their explanation of the geographical causes of such facts was not scientific. We can see, therefore, that the subject was in need of scientific data, of methods of research for this type of data, and of generalizations or laws gleaned from scientific research.

The first student to pursue scientifically the relationship of physical environment and man from a geographic viewpoint was Karl Ritter of Germany (1779-1859). As a student at Schnepfenthal, Ritter had been nurtured by the philosophy of his teachers, Salzmann and Gutsmuths. Salzmann had founded the school "to form healthy, reasonable, good and happy men, to mould them so that they would find resources of pleasure in themselves and be able to confer good upon their fellow-men."[6] This was the philosophy of Rousseau, and the foundation of the philosophy of the progressive thinkers of the day. Later as a young tutor, Ritter visited Pestalozzi at Yverdon, and there he adopted both a friend and his philosophy "that man is created by God and comes into the world possessing in germ all of the moral, physical, and intellectual powers which, if exercized and developed by the natural means the world offers him, will, by Divine grace, enable him happily to accomplish the destiny to which he is called."[7] It is not unnatural to find that Ritter developed a love for the truth, that he pursued truth for itself, and that he had respect for mankind, and above all, for his Creator. These qualities were evident throughout his long career as a teacher and writer.

Consequently, ignoring his predecessors, Ritter, by means of continuous observations of the earth, of man and of the Divine plan of the great Creator, set out to find the true relationship of nature and man. His ability to collect facts was stupendous, but he never lost himself in the woods of factual information, for he had the ability to generalize. Ritter brought man to the center of the geographical scene, for, without man, neither nature nor history would hold any interest for him. In his treatment of man as the central figure, he was influenced by his teleological philosophy, which became a vital factor in his conclusions. Geography to Ritter was "a statement of all divine laws, a revelation of God in nature and history, to be used in instructing youth to see and to trace the manner of working which the Deity follows." Ritter, however, used this philosophy to explain the facts of the world which he could not explain by his scientific knowledge: (1) "the uniqueness of the earth in the universe"; (2) "the earth as the home of that unique creature, man"; and (3) "the fundamental explanation of a host of geographical facts—the differentiation in character among the major land units of the world."[8] Ritter strove, as Hartshorne indicates, through the knowledge of the earth to understand the divine world, in the same way that the natural scientists were pursuing the thought of evolution. In regard to this teleological viewpoint, we must consider Ritter in the light of his time—we must remember that he lived before Darwin's evolutionary doctrines had given an order to great masses of scientific data.

Ritter is classed as a determinist, and as Ratzel and Semple attempted later, he set out to survey the influences of geographic environment upon the individual and society. Ritter felt that the influences of soil, climate, and topography were definitely pronounced among primitive groups, and that those peoples should be studied today. Since these primitive groups have evolved somewhat from their initial manners and customs, the influences of the environment are somewhat obscured. In the natural conditions of the country, he could see the past trends of history and he felt that by studying the physical conditions of primitive areas, the future direction of history might be predicted. He believed strongly in the influence of the environment on the characteristics of the inhabitants. "The very production of the soil has been interwoven into the texture of the human mind"; and at a glance, he could see the stamp of the occupations of peoples upon their feelings, thoughts, philosophy, and religious ideas.[9] Ritter, although a physical geographer, centered his research upon man; and, by so doing, set the stage for those who followed him.

Friedrich Ratzel (1844-1905), the founder of anthropogeography, was a natural link in the historic chain in the development of human geography. His forerunners—Humboldt, Ritter, Kohl, and Peschel—had laid the immediate foundation. These geographers, however, had other points of emphasis in their research. Ratzel, with his whole attention on anthropogeography, was able to make the first scientific investigation in this phase of the subject. Through his own preparation, he had brought to this field a background of the natural sciences, as well as philosophy, history, and economics. He had been inspired by the writings of Ritter, and he developed one phase of Ritter's work with greater precision and range of data. In addition to his scientific training, he, like Humboldt, was a world traveler; he had observed humanity in various natural habitats. He once summarized his career: "I traveled, I sketched, I described. I was thus led to *Naturschilderung* [description of nature]." Consequently throughout the years of his investigations, he collected innumerable facts and brought them together by deductive reasoning into "no less than twenty-four volumes and one hundred monographs and papers."[10] Thus by assembling facts of human geography from all over the world, he attempted to raise this body of subject matter to the rank of a science. His thinking was greatly influenced by Darwin's principles of evolution and Spencer's theories of sociology.

Groups of people, to Ratzel, were like organisms under the determining influences of environment. Being a cultural determinist, he considered man as a passive creature, and he directed much of his research toward finding the determining factors that shape the life of man. The earth seemed to have a living cover of humanity. In studying this "covering," he used three factors: (1) *Rahmen*, the geographic limits of certain groups of mankind; (2) *Stelle*, the situation or location on the globe; and (3) *Raum*, the space that a people occupies and in which it may expand. He considered the second factor, *Stelle*, to be of most importance, especially in the field of human history. Thus *Rahmen*, *Stelle*, and *Raum* constituted vital factors in the political progress of a group of people.[11] Ratzel saw "this living covering" of humanity all over the globe in the process of making history; he studied the great movements of peoples in their quest and struggle for space or *Raum*. He believed that a state experiences a complete transformation when it alters its area or when it is invaded by new tribes with a different culture. He observed that movements of peoples tend to proceed in the direction of needed resources, and usually toward their weaker neighbors. Topography, location, and direction of currents of streams were also considered as important factors in the direction of these movements. He realized, much more than any of his predecessors, that the development of the science of navigation was vitally important to the movements of peoples and to the exchange of culture. Ratzel considered the state as the highest form of organic life. To him, it was *Ein Stück Boden und Menschheit* (a bit of earth and humanity). He saw its gradual evolution, its transformation by new movements of peoples, its growth and overflow of its boundaries, its expansion into new land-areas, and its opposition to conquest by stronger neighbors.

Climate, he concluded, has a direct influence upon the bodily conditions, the mind and the character of man. Also, it has an indirect effect upon him by influencing conditions which are necessary for his existence. The groups of men living in the north temperate areas were judged to be superior in their political, military, and cultural achievements. Unfavorable and new climates, he observed, have detrimental effects, such as disease, mental inefficiency, and low energy. Similar geographic conditions in various parts of the world tend to cause a certain homogeneity of people. While he never went as far as Herbertson to classify these regions, yet he is given the credit for being "the founder of the diffusion interpretation of cultural transmission."[12] He made many studies that point out the differences as well as the similarities among peoples of various regions of the earth.

Ratzel's influence was extended to America by Ellen Churchill Semple, the exponent of his deterministic philosophy in this country, and one of the most distinguished of American geographers. No one knew better than Semple the weaknesses as well as the strength of Ratzel's work. Ratzel had covered extensive areas, collected data, made conclusions, but he had neglected classification and had failed to verify many of his generalizations. As Martha Krug Genthe has said so well: "He sowed his seed liberally for the use of anyone who would take care of it; he did not concern himself so much about planting it in regular rows." By this process of uncovering great quantities of facts and ideas, he laid a widespread foundation for his followers. "He made a trail in the jungle, and we who follow the trail may not blame him for unexplored corners of the forest."[13] His viewpoint in regard to man can be very clearly seen in a statement of Semple, expressed more poetically than Ratzel himself had expressed it: "Man is the product of the earth's surface. This means not merely that he is a child of the earth, dust of her dust; but that the earth has mothered him, fed him, set him tasks, directed his thoughts, confronted him with difficulties that have strengthened his body and sharpened his wits, given him his problems of navigation or irrigation, and at the same time whispered hints of their solution."[14]

The molding of geographical thought in France, as in no other country, has centered about one man,[15] Paul Vidal de la Blache (1845-1918), who directed this development while a professor at the École Normale Supérieure and at the Sorbonne. Vidal de la Blache had studied intensely the environmental theories of Montesquieu and Buckle, as well as the more general and extensive works of Humboldt, Ritter, and Ratzel. The works of Ratzel had gained quite an influence in France, particularly in the geographical thinking of Vidal de la Blache; but he, like Semple, felt that Ratzel's work needed further intensive study, and that his many generalizations needed testing. So the very important task of investigating and organizing this extensive field of subject matter of earth and man was begun. A number of studies of intensive research over small areas of France were worked out by the French Geographical School, which Vidal de la Blache had founded. Most of the geographers who worked on these monographs were the products of his teaching, had been trained in his lecture rooms, and had been educated with a background of the natural as well as the social sciences. Therefore, he set up an atmosphere of greatest freedom, since he felt that the science of human geography was immature and he believed that it needed as much free play of ideas as possible in order to develop the basic principles of the subject. His plan materialized; and for twenty years this method served as the basis for the reform projects and for the direction of geographic-social thought of the French geographers.[16] Toward the end of his career, he attempted to bring together the basic principles that had revealed themselves in his own research and in that of his fellow workers. These principles were published in a textbook, which contains his basic ideas of human geography.[17]

Vidal de la Blache is termed "an exponent of Possibilism," for he believed that the environment is full of possibilities, and that man, being a master of these, is the judge of their use. His research was directed toward the study of all the environmental causes of various responses and toward the study of man's behavior at various periods of history in the presence of many possible responses. The human groups which he studied in different localities seemed to be made up of different elements placed by chance in a certain environment. "No one knows what winds brought them together, nor whence, nor when; but they are living side by side in a region which has gradually put its stamp upon them."[18] Some of these groups had spent years trying to overcome certain obstacles of environment such as desert conditions; yet in time the collective experiences of the race seemed to help them overcome such conditions. Vidal de la Blache pointed out the uncertainty of climate. Man must play a game of chance with climatic conditions; but in this game with nature, scientific developments have made man more certain of his environment. He felt that man should be cognizant not only of the progress of his race, but also of the destruction caused by his occupation of certain areas. Man's experience should help to foretell something of his relationship to the earth at future periods of human history; and with science as man's aid, Vidal de la Blache could see great advancement for him in future periods. He did not agree with Ratzel and Semple that man should be regarded as putty in the hands of nature. He considered man as being both active and passive in respect to nature. His philosophy is well stated by his most distinguished pupil, Brunhes: "The man is there, the flint is there, but it is the man who makes the spark fly."

While Vidal de la Blache had investigated and attempted an organization of the subject matter of human geography, Jean Brunhes (1869-1930) refined still further the materials of the field, as he saw them, and developed a classification of this body of subject matter. Brunhes attempted to show, as scientifically as possible, the connection between two groups of elements: (1) the physical group—climates, soils, bodies of water, and types of vegetation; and (2) the human group—houses, roads, cultivated plants, domestic animals, and mineral resources used by man. He saw three sets of facts that should be of interest to man: (1) facts of unproductive occupation of the soil (houses, roads); (2) facts of plant and animal conquest; and (3) facts of destructive economy (animal, plant, and mineral exploitation). He considered these groups of facts to be the basic materials of human geography and related both to the earth and man.[19] The whole subject of races, with their customs and manners, he omitted from his classification, leaving them where he thought they belonged, with the subjects of anthropology and ethnology. In these two branches of knowledge, the connection between man and environment did not seem so apparent to him, but more involved with other factors.

Human beings were classed as "surface facts," and so were termed "geographical facts." Brunhes considered them as groups in towns or various habitations. He, like Vidal de la Blache, believed that man is both an active and a passive creature; for human beings tend to modify nature at the same time that nature is changing man. Since man alone, because of his intellectual ability, is able to modify to a great extent his environment, he believed that a much higher value should be placed upon man's accomplishments, as compared with those of plants and animals. Man replants forests, irrigates the desert, modifies the destructiveness of water, changes to some extent his climatic surroundings, cultivates plants in their proper environment, and uses domesticated animals where they are needed. Therefore, he uses his intellect and is an active creature. But he is also bound closely to certain physical phenomena. The rôle of salt, for example, has acted as a definite determinant of man in certain areas of the world. Water and gold, likewise, have determined many pages of human history. Certain geological formations have also played important parts, particularly in the early history of nations. The fall-line, the geological boundary between the coastal plain and the piedmont region, has played its part in the location of some of the chief cities of the eastern United States. Here men built towns, because of the break in transportation, and later reaped the economic benefits of the two adjacent areas. The location, configuration, structure of the land, and the climate, he thought, explained to a great extent the social evolution of a group.

As facts of major importance to mankind, he considered the completion of the Suez and Panama Canals of much greater value than the discovery of the North and South Poles. He always rated the material achievements of mankind much higher than the mere study of races and discoveries of uninhabitable areas of the globe.[20] He believed also that "our planet, successively or often simultaneously becomes different *to* us and *by* us";[21] that, accompanying the active and passive conditions on the earth, there is a psychological or "intermediary agency." In the early history of certain civilizations, because of certain geographic barriers, man had become a passive, intimidated creature; but as soon as these obstacles had been overcome, man's attitude became more affirmative. Brunhes stated two principles that man must recognize: (1) that all physical and human facts are in the state of change, that activity permeates everything; and (2) there is a relationship between all things, especially to the terrestrial whole. He used this idea of relationship in his statement on the nature of human geography, "a study of the relation between the various forms of human activity, economic, social and political, and the phenomena of physical geography."[22] Both Vidal de la Blache and Brunhes, by their intensive survey of the field of human geography, by their organization and classification of materials, made contributions toward the establishment of clearer relationships between man and his environment.

Andrew John Herbertson (1865-1915) believed firmly that "the more we know of the world the more we are filled with respect and admiration for our fellow-men, and the more we desire to be of use to them."[23] He was one of the chief exponents of Britain's world policy of broadening her geographic vision. Wolfgang L. G. Joerg, of the American Geographical Society, in his survey of the recent accomplishments of European nations in the field of geography, had noted: "In keeping with her traditional liberalism, Britain, more than any other country of Europe, it would seem, is making geography serve as a medium for the more sympathetic understanding of other peoples."[24] Herbertson's noteworthy contribution to the broad viewpoint of geography was his basic plan of organization, "the natural regions of the world," a presentation of systematic geography by which all facts could be assembled for study. He also gave geography one of its first textbooks with an economic emphasis: *Man and His Work: An Introduction to Human Geography*.

Vidal de la Blache had begun the study of regions with his monographs which concerned only small areas, most of which were in France. He made no attempt to find similar regions elsewhere; neither did he make any effort to classify regions. Herbertson believed that science should make progress in two directions: (1) it should move toward the causal rather than toward the accidental nature of facts; and (2) it should assemble these phenomena in larger and larger groupings.[25] Before the regional organization of Herbertson, the generally accepted plan was to begin the study of each continent from the geological facts of the topographic surface of the earth, and to continue with the physical laws that operate upon its surface. Finally the vegetation and animals, with man the last and least important factor, were presented. As this organization was followed for each continent, much material was duplicated. Herbertson developed a broader concept which embraced similar configurations, climates, soils, vegetations, animals, and human beings over the entire globe. He felt that if the peoples over the whole earth were linked up in their natural regions, geography and history would both take on a new meaning. A natural region of the world, according to Herbertson, should have certain similarities of configuration, climate, and vegetation. Human conditions were not important to him as a *basis* for these world regions, since man, moving from one region to another, is ever an unstable element.

In organizing his regions, he first studied the surface features, the climate, and the vegetation of the whole world. The boundaries were determined by oceans, mountains, and deserts. They were not to be considered as absolutely rigid lines, but as gradual "meltings" from one region to another.

After the surface features had been studied, maps of structural regions, climatic areas, vegetation, and rainfall were constructed. According to these maps, the earth was divided into seventy areas, basically climatic in structure. Finally, by the process of synthesis, there evolved six types of areas: (1) polar regions; (2) cool temperate regions; (3) warm temperate regions; (4) tropical desert, monsoon, and intertropical tablelands; (5) lofty tropical mountains; and (6) equatorial lowlands. These constituted Herbertson's *Natural Regions of the World*,[26] his major contribution to geographic organization.

Herbertson felt that such a classification had a direct bearing upon the educational process: it encouraged the use of the comparative method; it gave the student an incentive to think in terms of world-wide regional concepts. In this way, the student, learning the peculiar characteristics of each of the regions, would have a basis for comparison of land-areas, climates, vegetations, animals, and men. He could see his plan as a valuable aid to the study of history, as well as economics and political science, for developments in all these fields could be traced in the six regions. By this method he thought that very definite conclusions might be reached concerning the effect of environment upon mankind over the entire globe.

In working with these natural regions, Herbertson felt that he was not working with "sticks and stones," but with inorganic and organic matter, which exist together in very close relationship. The natural regions seemed to him as vital units, "a symbiosis on a vast scale." "It is more than an association of plants, animals and of men, it is a symbiotic association of all these, indissolubly bound up with certain structures and forms of the land."[27] Man's value fluctuates in the various regions. In the polar areas, he is relatively unimportant, while on the "Western Margins" of Europe, man is the center of all activity. Although man belongs in all of these regions, he is more important in some divisions than in others. When the geographer attempts to place man in a definite classification, or in an exact region, he finds great difficulties. According to Dryer, the greatest discord in natural regions arises in the case of man, who brings into his environment inherited, traditional, and imported characteristics which are not compatible with the natural region in which he is located at the present time.[28] Herbertson held a similar viewpoint concerning political divisions as basic elements of regional organization. Because of man's instability, he considered political boundaries as poor bases for classification. The most important accomplishment of Herbertson was that he discovered that the world *could be divided* into natural regions. His original work served as a foundation for later building in regional human geography. "It is only by persistent study and systematic development of regional geography that we can hope to understand the world-wide complex of land, water, air, plant, animal and man."[29]

Political strife in the middle of the nineteenth century closed the Academy at Neufchatel, Switzerland, and sent America four great scientists, one of whom was Arnold Henri Guyot (1807-1884). "It was for him falling in with the great geographical march of history, and coming to the land and people of the future, where no political or religious shackles were in the way of success." Although unfamiliar with the English language, Guyot accepted an invitation to deliver the winter course of scientific lectures at Lowell Institute in Boston. These lectures, given in French, were translated daily by Professor C. C. Felton of Harvard. Later, published as *Earth and Man*, these lectures became one of the most popular treatises of the period. The Lowell lectures and the published text established Guyot in America. He was soon in great demand as a lecturer and consultant of geographical problems. He met hundreds of teachers, especially when he served as lecturer of the State Institute of

Massachusetts. On this particular tour of the state, he was accompanied by his fellow countrymen, Agassiz and Krusi, who were lecturing on natural history and drawing. Thus the three European educators mingled professionally with the American theorists of this period, among whom were William Russell, Lowell Mason, and George B. Emerson. Later, in 1855, Guyot and Krusi were associated on the same faculty at the New Jersey State Normal School, where Guyot, a professor at Princeton University, was a visiting lecturer. The following statement attests the appreciation of Guyot's work: "The Trustees cannot speak too highly of the lectures of Professor Guyot. . . . There are few institutions of any kind in our country the students of which enjoy the advantage of a course of lectures so learned and at the same time so interesting."[30] While at Princeton, Guyot proved himself to be a man of great resourcefulness and a constant and indefatigable worker. He lectured. He developed the great museum. He went on summer field trips in order to become acquainted with the country. In addition, he published many texts and maps, which were of great value to teachers in every section of our country.

Guyot's greatest contribution to geography, however, was his book, *Earth and Man*, by which he gave America Ritter's concept of geography. The style of writing made his book very popular. Those who could not understand the profound statements of Ritter's books were inspired by the same ideas, expressed in simpler language by Guyot. In *Earth and Man*, he brought out the first important concept that he gave American geography. He declared that geography should be more than mere description of the earth. He wrote, "It should not only describe, it should interpret, it should rise to the how and the wherefore of the phenomena which it describes."[31] William Morris Davis believed that the rational or causal notion that was later stressed in our better geography teaching began with Guyot.[32] With this interpretation, geography could be developed as a science; while, as merely a descriptive subject, it had no chance for a scientific future. As a second contribution, Guyot presented a most convincing analysis of the superiority of the temperate climates as promoters of civilization. "In the temperate zones, all is activity, movement. The alternation of heat and cold, the changes of the seasons, a fresher and more bracing air, incite man to a constant struggle to forethought, to the vigorous employment of all his faculties."[33]

Guyot was also very much interested in the relationship of geography and history. Franklin Thomas in 1925 declared that Guyot's presentation, "although somewhat mystical and theistic," was the best that had been produced up to that date.[34] Guyot was the first to establish "a geographical march of history." He explained that the different continents had played different rôles in history. As Asia had been the cradle of civilization, Europe had been the first continent to play the rôle of civilizer. North America had received an imported civilization from Europe. He defined the "geographical march of history" by drawing attention to the fact that "the civilizations representing the highest degree of culture ever attained by man, at the different periods of his history, do not succeed each other in the same places, but pass from one country to another; following a certain order." *Earth and Man* described at length this march of history. He brought into the picture many facts of its occurrence, but he did not explain its causes, except as these were embodied in his teleological philosophy. Here we perceive his chief weakness, for he felt that the physical world must be explained in terms of the moral. Such statements as the following brought criticism: "It is correct to say that inorganic nature is made for organized nature, and the whole globe for man, as both are made for God, the origin and end of all things."[35] "We must elevate ourselves to the moral world to understand the physical world; the physical world has no meaning except by and for the moral world." But, as William Morris Davis wrote: "It is chiefly his teleological philosophy which we must give up, while we extend his physiographic base and his ontographic responses." We must consider Guyot's contributions and services to America, rather than his weaknesses.

Many have pondered over the question of Guyot's success, or lack of success in America. He was at Princeton "for a generation," where he occupied the only chair of geography of that period in our country. Although he had worked with thousands of teachers and students, yet he had no "distinguished follower" as most noted teachers such as Ritter, Ratzel, and Vidal de la Blache had developed in their classrooms. He was an indefatigable worker, as teacher, textbook writer, cartographer, and field worker. Richard Hartshorne thinks that his teleological explanations were responsible for his lack of a following. William Morris Davis, on the other hand, thought that, at his particular period, there was little demand for geographers—"that he was ahead of his time." Ellsworth Huntington thinks that his influence has been underestimated; that his teleological philosophy has been exaggerated out of its due proportion; and that his influence in American geography was more pronounced than that of Vidal de la Blache or Jean Brunhes. Perhaps Guyot came to this country at an unfortunate time; for not only the evolutionary theories of Darwin, but also the physical geography emphasis were in the ascendency. Also, a great proportion of his time was spent with teachers and students. In this type of work, degree of influence is very difficult to measure, unless one develops "an outstanding professional geographer." Teacher-education textbooks, however, praised his work very highly. Although not spectacular, Guyot had a widespread influence; and we would like to believe that "he was ahead of his time."

American geographic-social thought received, therefore, a European heritage that has been molded into the geographic philosophy of this country. The ancient social philosophers thought of life in terms of a powerful environment that determined even man's disposition and mental alertness, his energy and diseases, and his form of government. Climate was considered, even in early times, as the chief determinant of man's behavior. They had made observations, but had very little scientific data. For several decades, American textbooks defined geography according to the viewpoints of Carl Ritter and Arnold Guyot, his American exponent. These men influenced thinking by bringing man into the center of the geographic stage, and by constantly searching for man's true relationship to his environment. American students learned of Ratzel's philosophy through the teaching and writings of Ellen Churchill Semple, one of the greatest of American geographers. Although both Ratzel and Semple believed that man was mere putty in the hands of nature, and although they emphasized the environment to an extreme degree, yet their type of investigation was very profitable, if it is considered as a part of the chain of development of many decades. The writings of Vidal de la Blache and Brunhes, both well known in geographic libraries, are respected for the organization and classification that they present. Herbertson, with his broad world viewpoint, placed the foundation stones for later work in regional organization and systematic geography. These influences came to America mostly in the form of books. Indeed, Arnold Guyot, who had the distinction of being the first professor of geography in our country and the exponent of Ritter in America, was the only one of the European human geographers to live in this country. These, then, are the European influences which have contributed to the development of American geographic-social thought.

# Notes

# INTRODUCTION

1. F. M. Kircheisen, *Napoleon's Autobiography* (translated by Frederick Collins; New York, 1931), p. 241.

2. *The Social Contract,* Bk. II, Ch. IV. The original text has a sharpness of thought and a flavor which no paraphrase can capture:

"On doit concevoir ... que ce qui généralise la volonté est moins le nombre des voix que l'intérêt commun qui les unit; car dans cette institution, chacun se soumet nécessairement aux conditions qu'il impose aux autres: ....

Par quelque côté qu'on remonte au principe, on arrive toujours à la même conclusion; savoir, que le pacte social établit entre les citoyens une telle égalité qu'ils s'engagent tous sous les mêmes conditions et doivent jouir tous des mêmes droits. Ainsi, par la nature du pacte, tout acte de souveraineté, c'est-à-dire tout acte authentique de la volonté générale, oblige ou favorise également tous les citoyens; en sorte que le souverain connoît seulement le corps de la nation, et ne distingue aucun de ceux qui la composent. Qu'est-ce donc proprement qu'un acte de souveraineté? Ce n'est pas une convention du supérieur avec l'inférieur, mais une convention du corps avec chacun de ses membres: convention légitime, parcequ'elle a pour base le contrat social; équitable parcequ'elle est commune à tous; utile, parcequ'elle ne peut avoir d'autre objet que le bien général; et solide, parcequ'elle a pour garant la force publique et le pouvoir suprême. Tant que les sujets ne sont soumis qu'à de telles conventions, ils n'obéissent à personne, mais seulement à leur propre volonté: et demander jusqu'où s'étendent les droits respectifs du souverain et des citoyens, c'est demander jusqu'à quel point ceux-ci peuvent s'engager avec eux-mêmes, chacun envers tous, et tous envers chacun d'eux."

3. Robert Nathan, *Tapiola's Brave Regiment* (New York,

1941), pp. 136-137. Quoted by permission of the publishers, Alfred A. Knopf, Inc.

## THE DEFINITION OF THE GENERAL WILL

1. Jean J. Rousseau, *The Social Contract*, Bk. I, Chap. V.
2. C. W. Hendel, *Jean-Jacques Rousseau, Moralist* (2 vols., Oxford, 1934), Vol. I, Chap. V.
3. Rousseau, *A Discourse on the Origin of Inequality*, Preface.
4. Rousseau, *The Social Contract*, Bk. I, Chap. I.
5. *Ibid.*, Bk. I, Chap. VIII.
6. Rousseau, *Émile*, *passim.*
7. Rousseau, *The Social Contract*, Bk. I, Chap. II.
8. Rousseau, *A Discourse on Political Economy*, ¶¶10, 11, 12.
9. Rousseau, *The Social Contract*, Bk. I, Chap. VI.
10. *Ibid.*
11. *Ibid.*, Bk. I, Chap. VII.
12. *Ibid.*, Bk. II, Chap. IV.
13. *Ibid.*, Bk. I, Chap. IV, and Bk. III, Chap. I.
14. *Ibid.*, Bk. IV, Chap. VI.
15. *Ibid.*, Bk. II, Chap. VII.
16. *Ibid.*, Bk. IV, Chap. II.
17. *Ibid.*, Bk. II, Chap. IV.
18. *Ibid.*, Bk. II, Chap. III.
19. *Ibid.*, Bk. II, Chap. VIII.
20. *Ibid.*, Bk. II, Chap. XI.
21. *Ibid.*, Bk. III, Chap. XIV.
22. *Ibid.*, Bk. IV, Chap. II.

## NAPOLEON AND HITLER

1. *Correspondance de Napoléon I* (32 vols., Paris, 1852-1870), XXXII, 261.
2. *Ibid.*, p. 379.
3. *Commonweal*, XXXII, 379.
4. *New York Times*, April 9, 1939.
5. *Europe Under Hitler* (London, 1941), *passim.*
6. George Lefebvre, *Napoléon* (Paris, 1935), *passim.*
7. *Ibid.*
8. Statements of Napoleon to Roederer in 1801 and to the Council of State in 1805.
9. H. A. L. Fisher, *Napoleon* (London, 1922), Appendix.
10. *Correspondance de Napoléon* I, XVI, 166.

## IMPRESSMENT DURING THE AMERICAN REVOLUTION

1. Harrison to Speaker of the House of Delegates, May 6, 1872, *Official Letters of the Governors of Virginia*, H. R. McIlwaine, editor (3 vols., Richmond, 1926-29), III, 212-22.

2. *Rhode Island Session Laws, May 1777*, p. 29; *July 1777*, p. 8.

3. *The Statutes at Large, Being a Collection of all the Laws of Virginia, 1617-1792*, William W. Hening, compiler (13 vols., Richmond and Philadelphia, 1809-1823), X, 379-86.

4. *Ibid.*, pp. 413-16; *The Revolutionary Records of the State of Georgia*, Allen D. Candler, compiler (3 vols., Atlanta, 1908), II, 77-78; J. Reuben Clark, *Emergency Legislation passed prior to December 1917, etc.* (Washington, 1918), pp. 879-82.

5. *Journals of the Continental Congress, 1774-1789*, Worthington C. Ford, editor (34 vols., Washington, 1904-1937), III, 323-24.

6. *Ibid.*, VII, 144-47.

7. *Acts of the General Assembly of the Delaware State, etc. 1778* (Wilmington, 1779), pp. 13-16; *ibid.*, 1779, pp. 42-47.

8. *Session Laws of Pennsylvania, October 1777*, pp. 89-91.

9. Reed to Sullivan, May 21, 1779, *Pennsylvania Archives*, 1st series, Samuel Hazard, editor (12 vols., Philadelphia, 1852-56), VII, 427 ff.

10. William Duer, Statement, Mar. 9, 1779, *Letters of the Members of the Continental Congress*, Edmund C. Burnett, editor (8 vols., Washington, 1921-37), IV, 97-102.

11. Clark, *op. cit.*, pp. 737-38.

12. *Rhode Island Acts and Resolves Dec. 1778*, pp. 16-17.

13. Sullivan to Gov. of R. I., Jan. 5, 1779, *Records of the State of Rhode Island and Providence Plantations*, John R. Bartlett, editor (10 vols., Providence, 1863), VIII, 522-23.

14. *Rhode Island Acts and Resolves January 1779*, p. 9.

15. Hening, *op. cit.*, X, 496.

16. Harrison to Col. Armand, Jan. 3, 1782, McIlwaine, *op. cit.*, pp. 120-21.

17. Rutledge to Gen. Marion, Oct. 10, 1781, R. W. Gibbes, *Documentary History of the American Revolution* (Columbia, 1853), pp. 185-87. To one Col. Horry, Rutledge wrote: ". . . I assure you, that if I ever hear another complaint of the abuse of the press warrant which, confiding in your discreet exercise of it, I gave

you, I will instantly revoke it and never let you have another."—*Ibid.*, pp. 198-99.

18. *Laws of the State of New York, Commencing with the first Session of the Senate and Assembly, etc.* (Poughkeepsie, 1782), pp. 74-75, 105-6.

19. *Ibid.*, pp. 67-68; *Acts of the Fifth General Assembly of the State of New Jersey, At a Session begun at Trenton on the 24th Day of October, 1780* (Trenton, 1781), pp. 6-10.

20. Clinton to Capt. Townsend, July 10, 1780, *Public Papers of George Clinton First Governor of New York, 1777-1795-1801-1804* (10 vols., New York and Albany, 1899-1914), V, 952-53.

21. *Rhode Island Acts and Resolves, February 1780*, pp. 22-23; *Laws of New York*, pp. 287-88; *Acts of the General Assembly of the Delaware State, etc., October, 1783.* (Wilmington, 1784), p. 3.

22. Greene to Washington, Aug. 26, 1780, George W. Greene, *The Life of Nathanael Greene, Major-General in the Army of the Revolution* (3 vols., New York, 1867-71), II, 207-8.

23. John Lesher to Pres. Wharton, Jan. 9, 1778, *Pennsylvania Archives*, VI, 170-71.

24. Hening, *op. cit.*, X, 468-69; *ibid.*, XI, 79-81.

25. Genl. McDougall to Henry Laurens, Apr. 23, 1778, Library of Congress, Papers of the Continental Congress, no. 161, ff. 87-91; Greene to Pres. of Congress, Apr. 3, 1780, *ibid.*, no. 155, I, f. 216; Greene, *op. cit.*, II, 261-63.

26. William G. Sumner, *The Financier and Finances of the American Revolution* (2 vols., New York, 1891), I, 272-74.

27. Pickering to Pres. of Congress, Mar. 30, 1781, Papers of the Continental Congress, no. 192, f. 57.

28. Harrison to Pres. of Congress, Jan. 21, 1782, *ibid.*, no. 172, I, 332-35.

29. Washington to Dragoon Commanders, Oct. 25, 1777, *The Writings of George Washington*, John C. Fitzpatrick, editor (25 vols., Washington, 1931-), IX, 432-33.

30. Circular to the States, Aug. 27, 1780, *ibid.*, XIX, 449-51.

31. General Orders, July 4, 1781, *ibid.*, XXII, 327-28.

32. Washington to Genl. Gates, Nov. 1, 1778, *ibid.*, XIII, 191-92; to Genl. Greene, Dec. 22, 1779, *ibid.*, XVII, 300-1.

33. Washington to Brig. Genl. Irvine, Jan. 4, 1780, *ibid.*, XVII, 347-49; to Magistrates of N. J., Jan. 8, 1780, *ibid.*, pp. 362-65; to Officers, Jan. 8, 1780, *ibid.*, pp. 360-62.

34. Washington to Magistrates, Mar. 30, 1781, *ibid.*, XXI, 390-91.

35. Washington to Pres. of Congress, Dec. 15, 1777, *ibid.*, X, 159-60.

36. For example, see Livingston to Washington, Feb. 16, 1778, *Correspondence of the American Revolution; Being Letters of Eminent Men to George Washington*, Jared Sparks, editor (4 vols., Boston, 1853), II, 75-76.

37. Reed to Washington, July 15, 1780, *ibid.*, III, 15-28.

38. Washington to Gouverneur Morris, Dec. 10, 1780, Fitzpatrick, *op. cit.*, XX, 457-58.

39. Washington to Fielding Lewis, May 5, 1780, *ibid.*, XIX, 130-31.

## GARNER VERSUS KITCHIN

1. A. M. Arnett, *Claude Kitchin and the Wilson War Policies* (Boston, 1937), *passim.*

2. *American Mercury*, XLVII (1939), 1-8; *Congressional Digest*, VII (1928), 155; *Current History*, LI (1939), 7; *Harper's Magazine*, CLXV (1932), 669; *The Nation*, CXXXIV (1932), 465; CXLIV (1937), 722; CXLIX (1939), 139; CL (1940), 299; *The New Republic*, CI (1940), 266; XCVIII (1939), 277; XCVI (1938), 91; *North American Review*, CCXXXXIV (1932), 321.

3. George Milburn, "The Statesmanship of Mr. Garner," *Harper's Magazine*, CLXV (1932), 669-82.

4. Arnett, *op. cit.*, p. 15; Milburn, *loc. cit.*

5. Arnett, *op. cit.*, especially Chaps. V, VI.

6. Brief records of caucus meetings and tallies of votes are in the Kitchin Papers.

7. Oldfield to Kitchin, July 27, 1921. (The papers are arranged chronologically.)

8. Correspondence between Kitchin and Garner. There is a telegram, name of month illegible, filed as of August, which seems to have been sent June 29.

9. Oldfield to Kitchin, July 10, 1921.

10. Oldfield to Kitchin, July 22, 1921.

11. Kitchin to Oldfield, July 23, 1921.

12. Kitchin Correspondence, July 23, 1921, *et seq.*

13. Oldfield to Kitchin, July 27, 1921, and other correspondence thereabouts.

14. England to Kitchin, Aug. 2, 1921.

15. Kitchin to Garrett, Aug. 5, 1921.

16. Kitchin to Collier, Aug. 5, 1921.

17. Kitchin Correspondence, Aug. 8-18, 1921.
18. Kitchin to Oldfield, Aug. 18, 1921.
19. Oldfield to Kitchin, Aug. 11, 17, 18, 1921.
20. England to Kitchin, Aug. 23, 1921.
21. New York *Times*, Aug. 20, 1921. Cf. other dailies, same date.
22. England to Kitchin, Aug. 18, 1921.
23. Oldfield to Kitchin, Aug. 20, 1921.
24. England to Kitchin, Aug. 23, 1921.
25. A. R. Canfield to Kitchin, Sept. 6, 1921.
26. Garner to Kitchin, Oct. 5, 1922.
27. Milburn, *loc. cit.*

## THE ECONOMIC FUTURE OF THE SOUTHEAST

1. Table I

Total and Per Capita Income by States in the Region and for the United States, 1939*

| | Total Income | Per Capita Income |
|---|---|---|
| United States | $70,700,000,000 | $537 |
| Region | 6,326,000,000 | 300 |
| Alabama | 686,000,000 | 243 |
| Florida | 843,000,000 | 457 |
| Georgia | 905,000,000 | 292 |
| Mississippi | 441,000,000 | 203 |
| North Carolina | 1,068,000,000 | 302 |
| South Carolina | 508,000,000 | 268 |
| Tennessee | 856,000,000 | 296 |
| Virginia | 1,019,000,000 | 385 |

*Source: U. S. Department of Commerce, *Survey of Current Business*, October, 1940.

2. TABLE II

URBAN AND RURAL POPULATION IN THE REGION AND IN THE UNITED STATES, 1940*

| | Total Population | Urban Dwellers | | Rural Dwellers | | Rural Farm Dwellers | |
|---|---|---|---|---|---|---|---|
| | | Number | Percentage of Total | Number | Percentage of Total | Number | Percentage of Total |
| U. S.... | 131,669,275 | 74,423,702 | 56.5 | 57,245,573 | 43.5 | 30,151,076 | 22.9 |
| Region . | 21,102,935 | 6,820,589 | 32.3 | 14,282,346 | 67.7 | 9,171,215 | 43.5 |
| Ala....... | 2,832,961 | 855,941 | 30.2 | 1,977,020 | 69.8 | 1,339,197 | 47.3 |
| Fla....... | 1,897,414 | 1,045,791 | 55.1 | 851,623 | 44.9 | 303,762 | 16.0 |
| Ga....... | 3,123,723 | 1,073,808 | 34.4 | 2,049,915 | 65.6 | 1,366,025 | 43.7 |
| Miss...... | 2,183,796 | 432,882 | 19.8 | 1,750,914 | 80.2 | 1,402,549 | 64.2 |
| No. Car... | 3,571,623 | 974,175 | 27.3 | 2,597,448 | 72.7 | 1,651,197 | 39.3 |
| So. Car. .. | 1,899,804 | 466,111 | 24.5 | 1,433,693 | 75.5 | 913,448 | 48.1 |
| Tenn..... | 2,915,841 | 1,027,206 | 35.2 | 1,888,635 | 64.8 | 1,271,659 | 43.6 |
| Va....... | 2,677,773 | 944,675 | 35.3 | 1,733,098 | 64.7 | 923,377 | 34.4 |

*Source: *U. S. Census, 1940.*

3. In 1938 the birth rate in the United States and in the eight states was reported as follows:

United States 17.6

| | | | |
|---|---|---|---|
| Alabama | 21.4 | North Carolina | 22.9 |
| Florida | 18.6 | South Carolina | 21.9 |
| Georgia | 21.0 | Tennessee | 18.5 |
| Mississippi | 26.5 | Virginia | 19.8 |

A release by the Bureau of the Census, August 23, 1941, showed that the net reproductive rate for the United States for the five-year period, 1935 through 1939, was 96. A rate of 100 is required to maintain a stationary population if birth and death rates remain unchanged. The rates for the three major regions of the country were: South, 111; North, 87; West, 95. Of the eight states in this region, Florida alone was below the national average. The rates in the other seven states ran from 107 to 128.

4. In northern Alabama coal and iron deposits were more important reasons for industrial development.

5. It is significant that the inventor of the cotton gin, the machine that did more than any other one thing to fix slavery and the cotton economy on the South, was a visitor in the South from Connecticut.

6. This analysis of the mineral basis of an industrial region applies more to "heavy industry" than to "light industry." The latter may have considerable development away from the former, as our Piedmont and certain Pacific coast areas testify.

7. Chief reasons for the lower cost in Texas are fresher soils, larger farms, and more level land inviting more extensive use of machinery. The fact that Texas is farther from the markets for raw cotton is offset largely or entirely by the cheaper water transportation that carries the Texas crop to the markets.

8. The data on forests are taken from a pamphlet *The Southern Forest,* published by the Atlanta Field Office of the National Resources Planning Board.

9. TABLE III

DEVELOPMENT OF MANUFACTURES IN THE SOUTHEAST AND IN THE UNITED STATES, 1899-1939*

| | Number of Wage-Earners | Wages Paid (000 Omitted) | Value of Product (000 Omitted) | Value Added by Manufacture (000 Omitted) |
|---|---|---|---|---|
| Southeast | | | | |
| 1899...... | 429,847 | 111,160 | 574,547 | 268,545 |
| 1909...... | 658,628 | 224,962 | 1,232,173 | 550,895 |
| 1919...... | 814,203 | 709,539 | 4,122,068 | 1,720,353 |
| 1929...... | 962,563 | 777,268 | 4,910,368 | 2,350,534 |
| 1939...... | 1,036,645 | 776,532 | 5,204,313 | 2,138,123 |
| United States | | | | |
| 1899...... | 4,509,684 | 1,895,514 | 11,103,725 | 4,662,288 |
| 1909...... | 6,273,239 | 3,210,276 | 20,067,674 | 8,191,892 |
| 1919...... | 8,431,157 | 9,673,136 | 60,053,895 | 23,770,147 |
| 1929...... | 8,380,536 | 10,909,815 | 68,179,340 | 30,737,200 |
| 1939...... | 7,887,242 | 9,089,927 | 56,828,807 | 24,710,565 |

Source: U. S. Census of Manufactures.

10. In 1939, the rank of each of the eight states among the 49 (including the District of Columbia) in the United States in three aspects of industrialization was:

| *State* | *In Number of Wage Earners* | *In Value of Product* | *In Value Added by Manufacture* |
|---|---|---|---|
| No. Car. ............ | 10 | 12 | 13 |
| Ga. ............ | 14 | 20 | 20 |
| Va. ............ | 16 | 16 | 16 |
| Tenn. ............ | 17 | 18 | 17 |
| So. Car. ............ | 19 | 28 | 28 |
| Ala. ............ | 20 | 22 | 21 |
| Fla. ............ | 31 | 33 | 31 |
| Miss. ............ | 32 | 36 | 35 |

11. That considerable wage differences still persist between North and South in plants making various kinds of work clothing is shown in a recent publication of the Wage and Hour Division of the United States Department of Labor, *Statistical Material on the Single Pants, Shirts and Allied Garments Industry*, July, 1941. Lower wage costs as a primary factor in drawing industry to the South is emphasized in an article in *Fortune*, November, 1938, pp. 45 ff.

12. In the apparel industries a distinction should be drawn between those producing staple lines such as work clothing and hosiery and those producing fashion lines such as ladies' gowns and dresses. The staple lines may be expected to shift to locations where material and labor costs are favorable, whereas the fashion lines are tied more closely to style centers and markets.

13. Computed from annual reports of the Comptroller of the Currency.

14. Mississippi's movement under former Governor White to "Balance Agriculture with Industry" is the most prominent example in the region of governmental concessions to attract new industries. While public opinion in and out of the state is divided on the question of whether the experiment has proved to be wise, it is safe to assert that sound thinkers agree that if Mississippi is to have worthwhile industrialization, it must come because of fundamental attractions in the natural resources and labor supply rather than in subsidies.

## TWENTIETH CENTURY SOUTH-WIDE CIVIC AND LAY ORGANIZATIONS FOR HUMAN WELFARE

1. Conference material is based upon the several published reports. References in the *Readers' Guide* also were checked.

2. "Bishop Candler's Wail," *Independent*, LXXI (1911), p. 1101.

3. Edgar Gardner Murphy, *Problems of the Present South* (New York, 1905), pp. 5 ff.

## EARTH AND MAN

1. Hippocrates, "On Airs, Waters, and Places," in Francis Adams, *The Genuine Works of Hippocrates* (London, MDCCCXLIX), I, 181-222.

2. Jean Bodin, *The Six Bookes of a Commonweale* (translated

by R. Knolles; London, 1606). "The fifthe booke" contains environmental theories.

3. Montesquieu, *The Spirit of Laws* (London, MDCCL). Book II is concerned with geographical influences and man.

4. Henry Thomas Buckle, *History of Civilization in England* (New York, 1874), pp. 29-108.

5. Ellsworth Huntington, *Civilization and Climate* (New Haven, 1915), pp. 271-94.

6. William L. Gage, *The Life of Carl Ritter* (New York, 1867), p. 21.

7. Roger De Guimps, *Pestalozzi, His Life and Work* (New York, 1890), p. 407.

8. Richard Hartshorne, *The Nature of Geography* (Lancaster, Pa., 1939), p. 60.

9. Carl Ritter, *Geographical Studies* (translated by William L. Gage; Boston, 1863), p. 283.

10. Jean Brunhes, *Human Geography* (translated by LeCompte; New York, 1920), p. 32.

11. R. E. Dickinson and O. J. R. Howarth, *The Making of Geography* (Oxford, 1933), p. 198.

12. H. E. Barnes, and H. and F. B. Becker, *Contemporary Social Theory* (New York, 1940), p. 151.

13. A. P. Brigham, "Problems of Geographic Influence," *Annals of the Association of American Geographers,* V (1915), 3.

14. Ellen Churchill Semple, *Influences of the Geographic Environment* (New York, 1911), p. 1.

15. W. L. G. Joerg, "Recent Geographical Work in Europe," *The Geographical Review,* XII, No. 3 (July, 1922), 438.

16. Camille Vallaux, "Vidal de la Blache," *Encyclopaedia of the Social Sciences* (New York, 1935), XV, 251.

17. P. Vidal de la Blache, *Principles of Human Geography* (translated by M. T. Bingham; New York, 1926).

18. *Ibid.,* p. 17.

19. Jean Brunhes, *op. cit.,* pp. 48-52.

20. Jean Brunhes, "The Specific Characteristics and Complex Character of the Subject-Matter of Human Geography," *The Scottish Geographical Magazine,* XXIX (June 1913), 309.

21. *Ibid.,* p. 374.

22. H. E. Barnes, *The History and Prospects of the Social Sciences* (New York, 1925), Chapt. II, "Human Geography," by Jean Brunhes, p. 55.

23. John W. Adamson, *The Practice of Instruction* (London, 1907), Section III, "Geography," by A. J. Herbertson, p. 226.

24. W. L. G. Joerg, *loc. cit.;* Adamson, *op. cit.*, p. 194.

25. Adamson, *op. cit.*, p. 194.

26. A. J. Herbertson, "The Major Natural Regions: An Essay in Systematic Geography," *The Geographical Journal*, XXV (1905), 309.

27. A. J. Herbertson, "The Natural Regions of the World," *Address*, reported in *The Geographical Journal*, XLII (1913), 475.

28. Charles R. Dryer, "Natural Economic Regions," *Annals of the Association of American Geographers*, V (1915), 122.

29. *Ibid.*, p. 124.

30. *Report*, Board of Trustees, New Jersey State Normal School, 1855, p. 24.

31. Arnold Guyot, *The Earth and Man* (Boston, 1850), p. 21.

32. W. M. Davis, "The Progress of Geography in the United States," *Annals of the Association of American Geographers*, XIV, No. 4 (Dec., 1924), 165.

33. Guyot, *op. cit.*, p. 269.

34. Franklin Thomas, *The Environmental Basis of Society* (New York, 1925), p. 91.

35. Guyot, *op. cit.*, p. 29.

24. [illegible], [illegible] Ackerman, *op. cit.*, p. 394.

25. [illegible], p. [illegible].

26. A. J. Herbertson, "The Major Natural Regions: An Essay in Systematic Geography," *The Geographical Journal*, XXV (1905), 309.

27. A. J. Herbertson, "The Natural Regions of the World," [illegible] *Geographical Magazine*, XXIII (1913), 47.

28. Charles R. Dryer, "Natural Economic Regions," *Annals of the Association of American Geographers*, X (1920), 12[illegible].

29. *Ibid.*, p. [illegible].

30. [illegible], [illegible], New [illegible], [illegible] Normal School, 185[illegible], p. [illegible].

31. [illegible] Guyot, *The Earth and Man* (Boston, 1859), p. 2[illegible].

32. W. M. Davis, "The Progress of Geography in the United States," *Annals of the Association of American Geographers*, XIV, No. 4 (Dec., 1924), [illegible].

33. Ackerman, *op. cit.*, p. 290.

34. [illegible] [illegible], *[illegible] Geography* [illegible] (New York, 1827), p. [illegible].

35. Guyot, *op. cit.*, p. 10.